SUGAR GLIDERS
AS YOUR NEW PET

TS-269

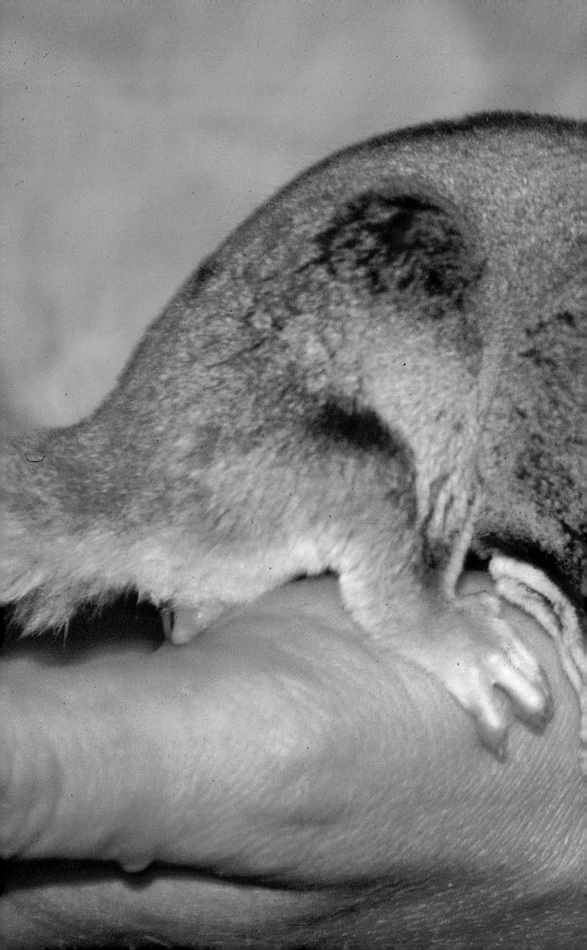

SUGAR GLIDERS AS YOUR NEW PET

By Dennis Kelsey-Wood

CONTENTS

Photography by Ralph Lermayer

© **1996 by T.F.H. Publications, Inc.**

Distributed in the UNITED STATES to the Pet Trade by T.F.H. Publications, Inc., One T.F.H. Plaza, Neptune City, NJ 07753; distributed in the UNITED STATES to the Bookstore and Library Trade by National Book Network, Inc. 4720 Boston Way, Lanham MD 20706; in CANADA to the Pet Trade by H & L Pet Supplies Inc., 27 Kingston Crescent, Kitchener, Ontario N2B 2T6; Rolf C. Hagen Inc., 3225 Sartelon St. Laurent-Montreal Quebec H4R 1E8; in CANADA to the Book Trade by Vanwell Publishing Ltd., 1 Northrup Crescent, St. Catharines, Ontario L2M 6P5 ; in ENGLAND by T.F.H. Publications, PO Box 15, Waterlooville PO7 6BQ; in AUSTRALIA AND THE SOUTH PACIFIC by T.F.H. (Australia), Pty. Ltd., Box 149, Brookvale 2100 N.S.W., Australia; in NEW ZEALAND by Brooklands Aquarium Ltd. 5 McGiven Drive, New Plymouth, RD1 New Zealand; in Japan by T.F.H. Publications, Japan—Jiro Tsuda, 10-12-3 Ohjidai, Sakura, Chiba 285, Japan; in SOUTH AFRICA by Lopis (Pty) Ltd., P.O. Box 39127, Booysens, 2016, Johannesburg, South Africa. Published by T.F.H. Publications, Inc.

MANUFACTURED IN THE
UNITED STATES OF AMERICA
BY T.F.H. PUBLICATIONS, INC.

WHAT IS A SUGAR GLIDER?

The sugar glider is the first species from the major group of animals known as marsupials to gain popularity as a domestic pet. The Greek word *mars* means a bag or pouch. This reveals one of the features strongly

members of the order do.

Since the sugar glider is a unique pet because of its zoological classification, it is worthwhile discussing the marsupials as a group. It is important that would-be owners

The sugar glider is one of the newest arrivals on the exotic pet scene. It is a member of the group of animals known collectively as lesser gliding possums.

associated with these animals– the possession of a pouch, or marsupium as it is more correctly known, into which the babies crawl at birth. Although some marsupials do not possess such a pouch, most well-known

should know as much as possible about the group to which the sugar glider belongs. Its effective management, particularly regarding reproduction, is guided by such knowledge.

AN OVERVIEW OF ZOOLOGICAL CLASSIFICATION

In order that every single life form could be referred to quickly, and without the risk of confusion, a system of nomenclature was devised during the 18th century by a Swedish naturalist, Carolus Linnaeus. It has been improved considerably since then, but in essence remains the same.

If you picture the system as a triangle, at the apex is a kingdom (that of animal life as compared with plants). This is divided into single (protozoan) or multicellular (metazoan) organisms. These, in turn, are divided into further groups based on collective features the members share. The process is repeated many times until eventually you arrive at the individual species lined along the base of the triangle. The term kingdom is a rank name. All its subdivisions also have rank or taxon names. There are subkingdoms, phyla (singular–phylum), classes, orders, families, genera (singular–genus), and species. There are actually many more ranks, such as superclass, subclass, infraclass, superorder, and so on, as well as those known as cohorts, tribes, and others. However, the first ones stated are regarded as obligatory in formal classifications; the others are used only in detailed texts.

At each rank, the members are

The sugar glider (*Petaurus breviceps*) is native to New Guinea and several nearby islands, the Bismarck Archipelago, and parts of Australia.

A distinguishing feature of the sugar glider is the dark stripe that extends from the nose down the length of the spine. Dark markings are also prominent around the eyes and on the legs.

grouped according to given features. We will commence at the rank of class, moving down the system until we arrive at the sugar glider. Popular examples of higher animal classes (those with backbones) are Aves (birds), Reptilia, Amphibia, Osteichthyes (bony fish), Chondrichthyes (sharks and rays), and Mammalia–the mammals.

Each of these groups contain members with shared collective features of their group, but all have a central backbone, breathe through gills at some point in their development, have well developed brains, senses, and so on.

THE CLASS MAMMALIA

There are some 4,500 species in the class Mammalia. They are characterized by the following key features.

1) All have a body covering of hair–this ranges from hardly noticeable, as in the whales and dolphins, to very evident, as in dogs, cats, bears, and others, including the sugar glider.

2) All breathe via lungs–even whales and dolphins must surface to take in fresh air, and expel respired air.

3) All give birth to live young which are suckled by their mother on milk produced by specialized sweat glands called teats, or mammae–thus the

name mammalia. There are two exceptions to the "live born" comment, these being the duck-billed platypus and the echidnas. These produce their offspring via eggs, but feed the hatched offspring via secreted milk.

4) All have complex blood circulatory systems in which

being cold-blooded, though the term more correctly means variable–it is controlled by the temperature of their environment. The mammals also share many anatomical features that collectively distinguish them from other classes of animals. Having outlined the main mammalian

A young sugar glider sampling a salad of fresh fruit. The diet of these pets includes a wide variety of foods.

the blood is maintained at a constant temperature. It is said to be homoiothermic (the same temperature), commonly known as warm-blooded. With the exception of the birds, all other animals are poikiothermic, or nearly so. They are known as

features, it would be normal in most other pets to proceed to the ordinal (order) levels of the class, because most pets have similar reproductive systems. This is not so with the sugar glider, so we must examine the subclasses first.

MAMMALIAN SUBCLASSES

Mammals, based on their reproductive organs, are divided into two types (subclasses). These are known as Theria and Prototheria. The latter subclass contains the single order of Monotremata, housing the egg-laying mammals just discussed. Theria is divided into the infraclasses of Metatheria, the marsupium (pouch). Here it attaches to a nipple, completing its development in this situation.

Other differences between the two types are that the placenta of marsupials is less well developed, the female reproductive tract is bifid, as is the male penis in many instances, and the gestation period is invariably shorter in

Sugar gliders are small, furry, and cute, with great pocket-pet appeal. However, they do have a few specialized needs. If you are thinking about purchasing one, you should first learn all that you can about their lifestyle and habits.

containing the marsupials, and Eutheria, in which the placental mammals are housed. A major difference between the two types is that placental mammals develop the embryo full term in the uterus. In marsupials it remains only a short period in the uterus before migrating to marsupials. Marsupials normally have more teeth than placental mammals. The lower jaw does not have the same number of incisors as the upper jaw, as in eutherians. There are a number of other anatomical differences related to marsupials but they need not be detailed here.

THE ORDER MARSUPIALIA

The infraclass Metatheria is divided into one order that contains the 280 species of marsupials. Not all zoologists agree on this situation. In some classifications, the marsupials may be divided into three to six orders when the criteria of reproduction alone is not the basis of defining an order. After all, eutherian placental mammals share a common reproductive system, but are divided into 19 orders. The marsupials are no less diverse than eutherian mammals. Only a few of the marsupials are well known to the average person.

These would include the opossums, wombats, Tasmanian devils, koalas, wallabies, and kangaroos. These are all popular zoo exhibits. Far less known are the many marsupial "mice," the native "cats" or quolls, the bandicoots, and the phalangers—which include the gliding possums within their numbers.

Given the rapid rise in pet popularity of exotic mammals, it is likely that a number of these lesser known marsupials will soon begin to attract growing attention. Indeed, the brush-tailed possum has a small following, though it's unlikely this will ever compare with the sugar glider in numbers.

The Family Petauridae

The marsupials are divided into

When fully mature, a sugar glider measures about 12 inches in length, half of which is its tail.

Sugar gliders are arboreal. In the wild, they easily get around by gliding from tree to tree and can exceed distances of 130 feet.

6-17 families, depending on the authority followed. Most accord the petaurids familial status (rank). For many years the members of this family, along with those of other families, were grouped within the much larger family Phalangeridae, the phalangers. Even the koala was placed in this family.

However, the petaurids are distinguished from the true phalangers on the basis of their genetic material (karyology), their blood composition (serology), and anatomical features. All petaurids are arboreal, meaning they spend most of their time living in trees. The 23 species in the family are housed in 6 genera. They are native to Australia, Tasmania, New Guinea, and a number of their offshore islands. They are commonly known as gliding, striped, or ring-tailed possums.

THE GENUS *PETAURUS*–THE LESSER GLIDING POSSUMS

We started our overview of classification with the common feature of life itself, at kingdom level. As we moved down the ranks, the members have become more and more similar in their collective features. At the genus level this is very apparent, members being obviously, and closely, related.

The genus *Petaurus* contains just four species:

1) *Petaurus breviceps*, the sugar, or honey, glider. Native to New

How good a pet your sugar glider will be is influenced by the attention and handling that it receives.

A young specimen. These animals are marsupials. Their gestation period is short, and their main development occurs when they are in the mother's marsupium, or pouch.

Guinea, its offshore island, the Bismark Archipelago to the east of New Guinea, and northeastern Australia.

2) *P. norfolcensis,* the squirrel glider. Native to eastern Australia.

3) *P. abidi,* the Papuan glider. Native to the Papuan coastal areas situated in southern New Guinea.

4) *P. australis,* the fluffy glider. Native to coastal Queensland, New South Wales, and Victoria.

THE SPECIES *PETAURUS BREVICEPS*

A species is loosely defined as a group of animals that, allowing for any sexual differences, display a very similar appearance. Further, they mate freely in their wild habitat to produce fertile offspring of their own kind. When individual populations of a species start to display minor, but constant, differences in their anatomy, physiology, or behavioral habits, they are defined as a subspecies.

They are examples of evolution in progress. In this text we are concerned only to species level. Not all authorities agree on the status of subspecies within the species *breviceps.* Marsupials are not primitive mammals. For many years it was the general belief that the marsupials were a rather primitive group of mammals. They were not especially intelligent, and were at an evolutionary disadvantage to the mainstream placental mammals of which they were early examples. Today, extensive studies suggest that the old view is incorrect.

Some authorities believe that the marsupials evolved in North America, moving south in the face of competition from the more advanced placental mammals. They migrated to Antarctica, thence to Australia before these land masses became separated. Once this happened, and with no placental mammals to compete with, they were able to proliferate–in Australia especially. The alternate theory is that the marsupials evolved in Australia spreading via Antarctica to South, then North America. However, when that latter continent split from Eurasia, it limited the potential for marsupial expansion into these other enormous continents. In other words, it was the timing of the continental shifts, rather than any inability to compete, that was the most important limiting factor on marsupials.

Where marsupials have been introduced to alien ecological systems containing placental mammals, they have proved equally successful. As examples, wallabies proved highly successful in New Zealand, southern England, Germany, and elsewhere. Southeastern American opossums were very successful when introduced into the western parts of the USA, having extended their natural range in spite of many placental competitors. If careful thought is placed into the reproductive strategy of the marsupials, there are numerous and obvious advantages over eutherian placental strategy.

The fact that the gestation period is short, and that the main offspring development is external to the mother's body, means the fetus is not such an incumbency on her when compared to a placental mammal in its later stages of fetal development.

If the fetus is lost (dead) for any reason, the marsupial will be in better physical condition than the placental female at the same stage of fetal development. She is more readily able to be mated again and have further offspring. Walker (1991) states, "This means of reproduction is perhaps more appropriate at this particular stage of marsupial development." Where studies of comparative intelligence have been made, the results suggest that many marsupials have greater learning capacity than some placental mammals. Others display a similar intelligence relative to their size. The marsupials are therefore best viewed as mammals that have developed a survival strategy eminently suited to their environment.

Facial characteristics include big, bold eyes and large, well-defined ears.

The cage must include furnishings that will enable your sugar glider to climb. Natural tree branches work well for this purpose.

DESCRIPTION AND LIFESTYLE

The sugar glider, *Petaurus breviceps,* has a typical body length of 12-16cm (4.7-6in) plus a tail of about the same length, giving a total length of 24-31cm (9-12in). Weight is in the order of about 135g (4.8oz) for a male, rather less for a female, even if she is of comparable size.

Its appearance is often likened to certain of the flying squirrels, whose conformation is somewhat similar. But squirrels are rodents, thus very different from the sugar glider in many of their characteristics and anatomy. The fur of the sugar glider is soft and silky. The head is somewhat wedge-shaped, the eyes large and round as befits a nocturnal creature. The ears are large and erect, enabling these marsupials to detect the high-pitched sounds of insects and similar invertebrates.

The tail is bushy. Along the side of the body can easily be seen the large gliding membrane that stretches from the front to the rear legs. During the breeding season, the females have a well-developed marsupium (pouch).

Housing that is easily accessed will make cleaning and other routine chores much easier.

There are five digits on each foot, all being clawed except for the inner opposable big toe (hallux) of the hind feet, which is adapted for grasping branches. The basic color is gray agouti, of varying shades of darkness on the back and sides. The underbelly, chest, and throat are white or cream. Facially, there is

LIFESTYLE

In their wild habitat, sugar gliders live in the trees of deciduous forests. They sleep during the day in nests sited in the hollows of tree branches. Leaves are gathered to line the nest. They are passed to the tail, which curls around them for transporting to the site.

A small plastic cylinder serves as a temporary nestbox for this youngster. Pet shops sell nestboxes that will be suitable for your pet.

a black stripe running from the nose to the nape of the crown. The eyes are ringed with black, this often extending to a complete circle of dark hair around the ears. The median facial stripe extends dorsally to the base of the tail.

Gliders live in family units comprising one or more males, females, and their offspring. They appear to be territorial, defending their family against other family units. As the unit gets larger, the mature young adults will leave and seek new partners from other

In conformation, the sugar, or honey, glider bears some resemblance to a flying squirrel. However, sugar gliders are marsupials, and squirrels are rodents.

units to commence new families. This ensures there is an exchange of genetic material.

Within the unit, recognition of fellow members is achieved by scents secreted from glands situated on the back and undersides of the male, as well as via his urogenital organs, and from glands in the marsupium of the female and her urogenital glands. Dominant males scent mark both their territory and their conspecifics. The diet of these animals is very cosmopolitan and omnivorous.

The latter means they consume foods of both plant and animal origins. Diet items include most invertebrates (worms, small spiders, and insects) together with any very small mammals they may come across, and the eggs of nestling birds. They enjoy the sap of some trees (especially eucalyptus), nectar, and flowering blossoms, as well as a wide range of fruits.

Travel is mainly via clambering among the branches of trees, and of course by gliding from one tree to another. But they also travel short distances at ground level before returning to the safety of high branches. The gliding potential of this species is said to be about 45 meters (148 ft). Much depends on the height from which they launch, and the prevailing winds. They are able to catch flying insects as they glide. They can change the direction of their

The gliding membranes extend from the outside of the front feet to the ankles.

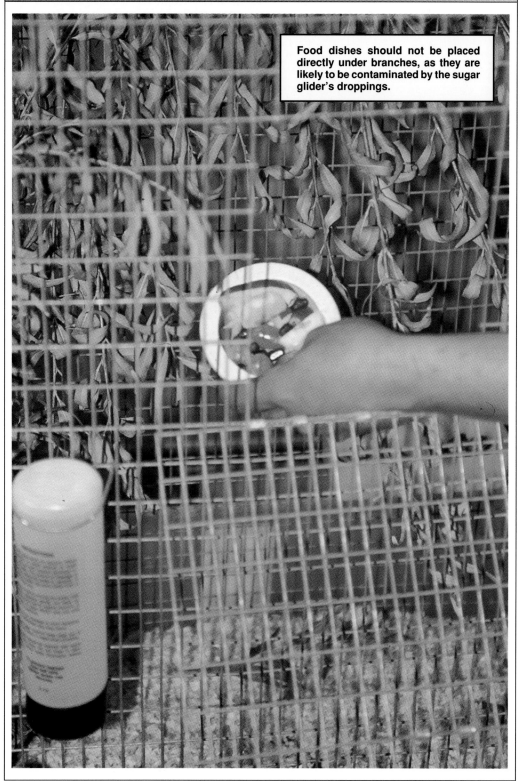

Food dishes should not be placed directly under branches, as they are likely to be contaminated by the sugar glider's droppings.

flight by adjusting the tautness of their gliding membrane on one side of the body by movement of the appropriate front and rear feet. The tail is also used to assist in directional movements.

When landing, they arch their back and bring their outstretched legs into their normal positions. This results in the gliding membrane acting rather like a brake to slow down the speed. Sugar gliders have numerous natural enemies, the most obvious being snakes, raptors (birds of prey), rodents, and, of course, humans. Longevity is excellent considering their small size. Under captive conditions, 14 years has been recorded. In the wild it will be rather less than this because few wild animals ever die of old age. Maturity is normally attained late in the first year, or early in the second year, of their lives.

THE DOMESTIC SUGAR GLIDER

Although the sugar glider is a relative newcomer to the American pet scene, it has been kept in private homes and zoological collections throughout the western world for many years. Between 1865 and 1937, twenty-two babies were born in London Zoo. Many other zoos have featured the species, and its relatives, in their nocturnal houses. In Australia, sugar gliders were popular pets in the pre-1960 days. They were often called flying squirrels. However, the strict laws enacted by the

In the wild, sugar gliders live in tree hollows. Domesticated members of the species need a safe, secure place to which they can retreat during the day.

A food dish of this design is ideal. It can be attached to the side of the cage, where the pet can gain easy access to it. Additionally, there is less chance that the food will be fouled by waste material.

Australian government in 1959 to protect their natural flora and fauna dramatically curtailed this situation. It also means the gliders available to the pet trade are not Australian in origin, exports being banned in 1959. They are from other parts of their distribution range.

NOMENCLATURE

Although not essential for the pet owner, other than as a point of interest, it is useful for the serious breeder to understand why all animals are given scientific names, as well as common names. The problem with the latter is they are not regulated in any way. This means that many names can, and often are, applied to the same animal, and that the same name may be used for other animals. You have seen that the sugar glider is also called a honey glider, but it was also popular under the name of flying squirrel in Australia, a very misleading name. Yet another synonym is the short-headed flying phalanger. In other languages it has other names. It will readily be appreciated that such a situation can create considerable confusion.

Scientific nomenclature overcomes this situation because each living organism has its own unique name. The system used by zoologists is called the binomial system of nomenclature. It is based on Latin, but a number of other languages are used in it. The name is created by stating the genus of the animal, then applying a species or trivial name to this. The trivial name is always treated as an adjective, even if it is a proper noun, as with a person's name. The genus always commences with a capital letter, the trivial always with a lower case; there are no exceptions. Only when these two names are used together is the animal uniquely identified. The scientific name normally appears in italics or in a typeface different from that of the main text. This only applies to the genus and ranks below this (species and subspecies).

The name *Petaurus* means a sort of springboard used by acrobats (who fly through the air)

At the present time, there is no housing designed especially for sugar gliders, but there are suitable options available. The indoor aviary shown here affords its occupant ample room for movement.

in Latin, while *breviceps* means short-headed. The name that often appears after a species or genus name is that of the person who first applied it. The date this was first published usually appears after this name. In the case of the genus *Petaurus*, this was by Shaw and Nodder in 1791. When a subspecies is given recognition, the trivial name of the type on which the species was named is repeated to create a trinomial. This becomes the nominate form–the type on which the species was based. The subspecies has its own unique trivial added to the species name.

For example, *Petauras breviceps breviceps* is the nominate form of this animal. *Petaurus breviceps papuan* is the subspecies from Papua. Serious hobbyists should be familiar with scientific nomenclature because it is used extensively in zoological texts.

HOUSING

When considering the housing needs of any pet animal, a number of factors must be taken into account. After listing these we can discuss them with specific reference to the sugar glider.

1) It should be as spacious as possible, reflecting the amount of time the pet is allowed out of its accommodations to exercise.
2) It should be so constructed that it can be readily accessed and cleaned.
3) It should be secure, so the pet cannot escape when the owner is absent.
4) It should be very safe with no sharp metal projections which could injure the pet.
5) It should be sited where its temperature will remain reasonably constant, not subjected to rapid fluctuations of heat or cold.
6) It should be furnished in a manner that will provide the pet the opportunity to amuse itself when the owner is not present.
7) It should be provided with adequate sleeping, feeding, and drinking facilities.

The sugar glider uses its long furry tail to aid in directional movement when it is gliding. In the wild, the tail is also used to transport nesting material, such as leaves, to the nest.

CAGE STYLE & SPACE

At this time there are no commercially made accommodations for sugar gliders. It's a case of adapting those produced for other animals. The arboreal lifestyle of these pets is such that the most appropriate housing will be a large bird cage or indoor aviary, the latter being especially recommended for the pet that must spend some hours at a time in its accommodations. Sugar gliders are very lithe animals which can easily escape from cages unless they are constructed using a weldwire mesh with a hole size of no more than 2.5cm (1in) square for adults, smaller if babies are present. The alternative is a cage made for finches, where the distance between the bars is narrow. The cage will ideally be taller than it is wide, because sugar gliders prefer to rest a good distance from the floor. This gives them a natural sense of security, as is the case with avians.

Modern cages are made in a considerable range of sizes and materials, including epoxy- and plastic-coated weldwire, chromium-plated wire, and plain galvanized wire. The galvanized wire is the least expensive. You can purchase weldwire panels which can be assembled to form any cage size you wish. Indoor aviaries are available in a range of sizes and materials, often coming complete with small wheels so

The sugar glider is not as smart as some other pets, but it does have enough appeal and charm to make it interesting to keep.

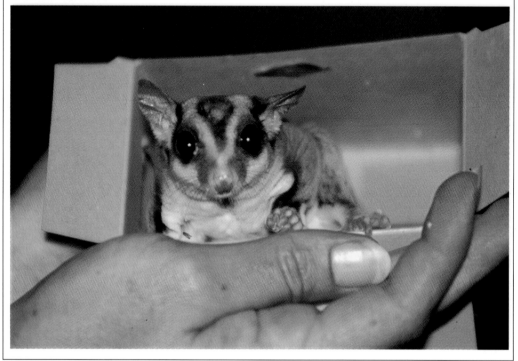

The amount of time that it takes a sugar glider to become acclimated to its owner can vary. It may be just a few hours, or it may take a number of days.

they can readily be moved from one site to another. These are perfect for small breeding family units of sugar gliders, and can be furnished in a most attractive manner.

When choosing a cage, consider how readily it can be accessed for cleaning. In some instances, the entire wire part can be lifted from its plastic base. In others, there may be a pull-out drawer for removal of fallen foods and fecal matter. Another variation is where an entire side can be lowered to form a platform. This may also have an access door for use when the side is not lowered. The more easily accessed, the more easily

cleaned and furnished. Some cages are fitted with an external apron that will channel fallen food or floor material back into the base of the cage. This saves unsightly droppings on the carpet. It is certainly worth visiting several stores to see the range available.

THE BREEDING ROOM

The potential breeder should use cages recommended for small parakeets or finches. These flight cages and aviaries are either floor to ceiling, or half flights under which other needed items can be stored. By connecting these to outdoor flights, the sugar gliders can gain obvious benefits during the warmer months. When flights share a common wire wall, it would be prudent to double wire this so the residents on either side cannot reach each other through the wire by biting each other's feet.

When designing a breeding room, be sure to feature ample ventilation or pathogenic (disease causing) colonization and proliferation will occur. The use of one or more ionizers will be beneficial in reducing bacterial build-up, as well as minimizing odors. Ionizers can be obtained from all good pet shops and bird supply specialists. They are economical to operate. They function by releasing millions of negative ions that attract airborne dust and bacteria which fall to the ground, or onto surfaces, where they are readily wiped clean. Dust extractors serve a similar function.

The use of a rheostat on the lighting is another useful feature in a breeding room. It controls the

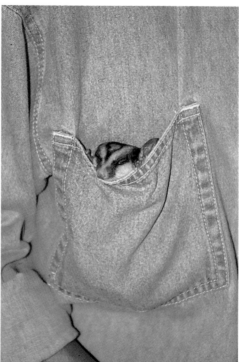

A shirt pocket is a cozy spot in which to take a nap. Part of the appeal of sugar gliders is their small size. Males average around 4½ ozs.; females weigh somewhat less.

intensity of lights, bringing them on slowly, so the gliders are never startled by lights suddenly going off or coming on. Being nocturnal, these pets will appreciate the use of specialized lighting overnight that is biased to the blue or red ends of the spectrum. Finally, when designing a breeding room, be sure to allow more working and storage space than you think you will need. Lack of space really does create extra work in cleaning and routine management; it also results in the room rapidly becoming untidy.

SECURITY

Your pet should not be able to unfasten the latches in most modern cages. However, you might ponder the cages' features safety from the viewpoint of a small child. Select a model that such a youngster cannot access easily or you might risk losing your pet. Check cages for sharp projections which could cause injury to your sugar glider. The more costly units will be well

The best pet sugar glider will be one that has been domestically bred and socialized at a young age.

finished. Those at the lower end of the price range are not always as safe and secure.

LOCATION OF THE CAGE

It is very important that the cage is not placed where it will be exposed to drafts or intense direct sunlight. It should not be placed over heaters or coolers that would create sudden temperature fluctuations as they turn on or off. The ideal location will be a shaded spot in the room away from a heater or air conditioner. These are nocturnal animals that dislike strong sunlight. To become well socialized to your family, they should be in a room where you spend much time, other than the kitchen, which is a potentially

fatal environment for your pet.

The kitchen, with its electric or other cooker hobs, boiling pans, extractor fans, electrical appliances, and sharp knives, is no place for your pet. There are additional health hazards of the pet fouling surfaces, or gorging on food items. The cage should be so placed that when they are in their nestbox, or on a high branch, your pets should be level with, or just above, your head height. This helps reduce the stress factor that can be a problem in timid creatures, which these are, especially when newly acquired. The more they see of you, the less timid they will be. The comfort temperature range of 65-75°F (18.3-24°C) needed for these pets

Sugar gliders are very inquisitive animals and will enjoy exploring their environment.

Young sugar glider at play. Sugar gliders like to crawl into small spaces and small places.

is much the same as your own. Below the stated minimum they may become chilled. Too much above the maximum could result in heat stress, especially if ventilation is not adequate in confined spaces, such as breeding rooms.

Rapid temperature fluctuation should always be avoided. Most animals can tolerate a few degrees of change over a 24-hour period. They can adjust to cooler or warmer heat levels over longer periods. Sudden change results in health problems. With this in mind, do check the temperature range in the seller's accommodations. This should be maintained initially, then adjusted over a period of one or two weeks if this is deemed desirable.

CAGE FURNISHINGS

Under this heading comes perches and floor covering. Sugar gliders are agile and active climbers. Their furnishings should reflect this. Depending on the size of the accommodations, you can feature natural tree branches, such as apple, pear, willow and other safe woods, small platforms made of timber or plastic, as well as any of the many commercially made perches, such as those for parrots.

A sugar glider that is let out of its cage to roam freely in the home should be supervised at all times so that it does not injure itself.

There are many ways you can arrange these items, but the following are practical considerations to observe.

1) Do not overcrowd the cage with branches so there is limited open space for the pets.

2) Do not place branches or perches directly over food or water pots, as the food and liquid could become fouled. Place them alongside such dishes.

3) If food and water pots are placed on the cage bars, ensure that your pet can easily reach them from its branch or perch.

4) Replace natural branches as they are denuded of bark. The best choice for floor covering is granulated paper, sheets of non-printed paper, or natural wood pulp. Pine shavings are a popular choice, but in recent years these have been linked with potential problems that are worthy of comment.

Cedar, white pine, and ponderosa pine contain phenols. These compounds are acidic and potentially dangerous to small animals. They affect the lungs and liver. In the former they constantly irritate the nasal passage, thus increasing the potential for bacterial attack. In the liver they place a heavy load on its blood filtering capacity. Once the liver is unable to filter out the phenols, it becomes far less effective. Further, it appears that the phenols depress the immune system, inducing conditions typically seen in older animals. In short, the phenols reduce the life expectancy of the animal. Softwoods are more readily available as bedding than hardwoods and are less costly. However, the growing data linking pine with health problems is such that more breeders and owners are playing safe and avoiding it. Indeed, cedar is specifically outlawed in Colorado as bedding for small mammals and cage base material.

Most of the research done on this bedding material stems from observations made of rabbits, guinea pigs, rats, and mice. At this time the North American Hedgehog Association is commencing a project to look into the effect of bedding on these pets, given that white pine is by far the most common for that exotic mammal. The use of sawdust is not recommended, not only because most of it is from softwoods, but also because it clings to food items. It can become ingested, increasing its potential danger. Clay or clay-based cat litters should also be avoided due to the silica dust they contain, which may also cause respiratory problems, as well as cancer.

NESTBOX AND FEEDING RECEPTACLES

Your sugar glider needs a cozy nestbox in which to sleep. This

Accommodations should be roomy—the more space the better.

can be made from various materials and must be easily cleaned. If wooden, it should be well painted inside with a washable non-lead-based paint. Alternatively, and even better, would be to use one of the laminated boards. Another possibility is a one-gallon plastic need not be enormous–just large enough for the pet to enter. It can be placed to one side of the box. The nestbox size should be of the order 15x15x23cm (6x6x9in), or a little larger if you have two or more of these pets. The nestbox should be lined with granulated paper, commercial nesting

When you first bring your sugar glider home, give it time to adjust to its new environment. Don't overhandle it.

tote box, or even a one-gallon milk container in which one side is strengthened as a floor. A parakeet nesting box is yet another possibility–visit your pet store to see what they have. Small mammal nestboxes are now being commercially made.

Whatever the choice, it will need a suitably sized access hole. This material for small mammals, or wood pulp. Avoid hay because the pet will urinate in the nestbox. This could prompt fungal spores to develop if they are present in the hay.

The nestbox should be sited quite high up in the cage. As with birds, the position it faces can be of some importance at breeding times.

A sugar glider should be handled gently but securely. Some sugar gliders are more amenable to handling than are others.

Some individuals can be rather selective; others seem unconcerned. The choice of water vessel is between inverted bottles of the hamster type, or open pots hooked onto the cage bars, placed on an elevated feeding platform, or at floor level. From the hygiene viewpoint, it is better these items are elevated. It reduces the risk of their being contaminated with either fecal matter, or floor covering material.

Although inverted bottles are both hygienic and labor saving, this author prefers open dishes. They are a far more natural method for drinking, and they require that you replenish them daily so the water is always fresh. One of each would be a nice compromise, and you can see which is the preferred choice. Food vessels can be hooked on parrot feeders, or pot dishes placed on an elevated feeding platform. You will want one for dry foods, and one for moist or softfoods.

Finally, it is better to obtain your housing in advance of the sugar glider. By so doing you give yourself the opportunity to carefully review the locally available range. If this is not what you want, your pet dealer may be able to special order for you. You can also send for catalogs from bird cage/flight specialists that advertise in the birdkeeping magazines sold by your pet shop. Housing is very important; if it's a rush purchase, chances are high it will not be exactly what you wanted.

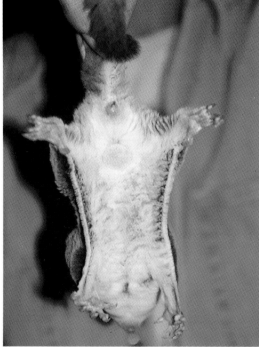

The gliding membranes are easily visible when the animal is viewed from its underside.

ROUTINE CLEANING

The size of the accommodations, and number of sugar gliders, will dictate the number of times the cage needs cleaning. Food and open water pots should be washed daily. Fecal matter should be routinely removed daily, and the entire floor covering replaced each week.

The cage bars must be cleaned on a very regular basis, as should all perches, platforms, and branches. The best cleaning agent is a diluted solution of household bleach. However, when used for complete cage cleaning it must be thoroughly rinsed away to ensure there are no residuals. Disinfectants contain phenols, so it is important to rinse these from any items they are used to cleanse. Be especially diligent in cleaning bars and branches on which the pets rub their snouts. This is one of many ways in which pathogens are transferred from these surfaces directly to the mouth and nasal passage. Chipped and cracked feeding utensils should be replaced immediately.

Breeders should ensure fouled floor material is not stored in the stockroom, but removed and disposed of as it's gathered. It is wise for this group of enthusiasts to have a number of spare cages and flights. Stock can be routinely rotated so that each cage or flight is stored after being thoroughly sterilized. Thus you minimize the potential for pathogenic build-up that is ever present if cages are in continual use.

Breeders should have some facility, away from the main stock, that can be used to quarantine newly acquired gliders, and any that may be unwell.

It cannot be overstressed that attention to routine cleaning is your most important safeguard against health problems. It is also the easiest husbandry chore to be neglected, or put off until another day.

The cage—including the bars—and its furnishings must be cleaned regularly.

LIVING WITH A SUGAR GLIDER

The sugar glider has instant "cuddly" appeal that makes people want to own one. However, like any pet, considerable thought should be given to all its characteristics before the decision to obtain one is made. If this was done by more potential owners, there would not be the high number of abandoned pets or those that, after an initial novelty period, are relegated to sad neglected lives in small cages. All too often, would-be owners focus entirely on the endearing features. They will totally overlook any negatives. Only later, when these

are blatantly apparent, do they begin to give them thought. It is appropriate that you fully understand what owning a sugar glider means in terms of a commitment to the animal. If you are satisfied that the potential negatives will not be a cause for concern, you will become a delighted owner.

POTENTIAL SUGAR GLIDER PROBLEMS

First, you should never purchase one of these pets simply because a younger member of the family wants one. Parents who do

A sugar glider will relish fresh fruits, which should be a regular part of its diet. Any fruit that is given should be of good quality, free of spoilage.

These animals are omnivorous, which means they eat plant and animal matter. It is not difficult to provide a nutritious, appealing diet for them.

this, and expect the child to retain their interest and care for the welfare of the pet, are not being responsible adults. Some children soon lose interest in their pets, then want something else. As a parent, you must accept this reality and be prepared to take over the management of the sugar glider. In other words, if you are not fascinated by these little marsupials, it would be better not to have one in your home. You cannot gamble on whether or not it will receive the care and attention it will certainly require.

If you are an extremely houseproud person, you must think in terms of a large indoor aviary for the sugar glider, or not have one at all. These are active little mammals requiring plenty of space in which to exercise. The caged pet should be given liberal out of cage time. This means it will get into a certain amount of mischief. For example, it can easily climb to high points, then launch itself across part of the room. It may land on a shelf, or cupboard, knocking ornaments over. It may also clamber up drapes, defecating on these. It may chew on soft furnishings, and will happily take every opportunity to search for food items.

It is important that the housing for your pet sugar glider is kept scrupulously clean. Males, especially, scent mark their territory. While the odor is not as unpleasant as that of dogs, cats, or ferrets, it may still be offensive to some people. Another important consideration is that if you keep cats, ferrets or dogs, the former two in particular, the glider must be very carefully supervised when out of its cage. Cats and ferrets regard it as a small furry animal to be chased–a potential prey. Rabbits and guinea pigs will not be a problem if both are roaming in a room, but parrots could be. The medium to larger ones could inflict a painful wound on a sugar glider landing near them.

Likewise, small children could easily hurt one of these delicate little animals if they handled it too roughly–they may also receive a sharp nip as a result. You cannot teach a sugar glider to do tricks as you can a dog or a parrot, nor will it litter train like cats. Finally, you will be able to exercise this pet in your yard only if you have a totally wired flight.

SUGAR GLIDER VIRTUES

The sugar glider is an extremely endearing animal that will appeal to those wanting a pet that is unusual, amusing to watch, and very companionable. Its intelligence is not on a par with dogs or cats, but it is sufficient to make it interesting. It will come to know each member of your family, responding positively to gentle handling. As a breeding proposition, the sugar glider has its advantages as it is not a prolific producer. This means that you will not be overrun with surplus offspring. In due course, color mutational forms will appear. These will create instant extra interest in these pets.

Gliders are economical to keep, most of their favorite food items being found in the average kitchen. They are very hardy if maintained in clean conditions. They do not appear to suffer from any major health problem. Their life expectancy (in excess of ten years) is excellent for such a small mammal. Being nocturnal, the sugar glider will tend to be most active during the evening when you are at home. However, they can adjust to daytime activity, as long as you avoid placing them in bright light. Like any pet, the sugar glider may not be suited to every person or family. However, if you carefully evaluate its potential problems and virtues beforehand, you should be very satisfied.

BONDING

Just how well your sugar glider becomes an enchanting pet will be exclusively determined by how well it bonds with you and other people. For this reason it is always best to obtain a domestically bred youngster. It should have had no bad past experiences with humans to affect its behavior. When first obtained, leave the pet for a few hours to explore its new home, and generally recover from the trauma of being moved from its former home. Next, it should be offered tidbits to tempt it to come to the cage bars. After this you can place your hand in the cage to offer food morsels. Your objective is to steadily win the confidence of the pet so it has no fear of your hand or your size.

This process may take only hours, or it could take days. Do not attempt to rush this all-important stage. Once it is happy being near or on your hand, you can stroke and gently touch all parts of its body. At this stage, the pet is ready to be given room freedom. Should it become fearful of something, it will regard your hand as a place of safety. From this point onward it is merely a case of

When it is first handled, it is not uncommon for a sugar glider to produce vocalizations that can be quite high-pitched and loud.

very regular and gentle handling until it will happily sit on your shoulder, arm, or lap as you watch TV or read a book.

You will be able to move around and it will come with you, maybe leaping from your shoulder to some other vantage point—then back to you when you call its name and offer it your arm.

Always supervise matters when young children are handling the pet. They can forget how easily it can be hurt. This may make it both nervous and potentially aggressive. Never let toddlers hold the pet, only stroke it when in your hands.

SECURITY MEASURES

Be sure to safeguard against the possibility of your pet launching itself and crashing into a glass window! This is most likely during its first few outings from its cage. Either hanging plastic mesh, or closing the drapes, is recommended at this early stage. Always use a screen to protect open fire grates. Aquariums should be fitted with a hood so your pet cannot glide into the water. Keep all electric wires as tidy as possible. Do remember to keep windows and doors closed when the pet is free roaming. It is wise to remove fragile ornaments from shelves. Be sure indoor plants are not toxic to these pets. Sugar gliders are very inquisitive pets. Be sure cupboards, especially if they contain food items, are securely closed. Never leave poisonous substances where the pet might access them thinking they could be food items. It is wise to walk around the living area and try to envisage what mischief, or danger, you could get into if you were a sugar glider!

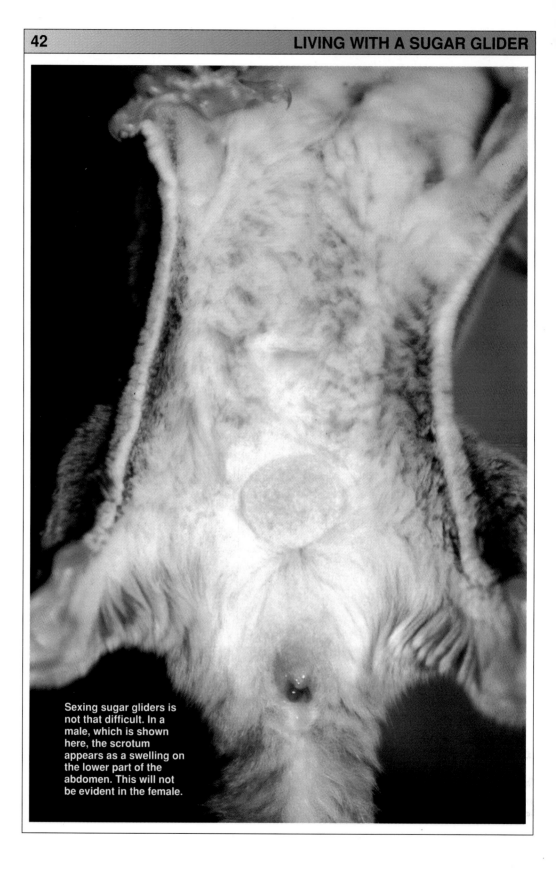

Sexing sugar gliders is not that difficult. In a male, which is shown here, the scrotum appears as a swelling on the lower part of the abdomen. This will not be evident in the female.

CHOOSING A SUGAR GLIDER

After you have decided that you would like to own a sugar glider, you must find out whether it can legally be kept in your state and locality.

The other considerations that should influence your choice are the following five factors which are discussed as listed.

1) The source
2) Age
3) Pet or a breeding individual
4) Assessing health
5) Cost

THE SOURCE

Sugar gliders are at this time still being caught and imported from the wild, which is no longer necessary as there is an ample supply of domestically bred stock. There is no perceptible price difference between the two types of gliders, so you are strongly advised to obtain a domestically bred individual. Such a pet has many advantages over its wild counterpart. You can establish its exact age. It will be far less stressed, less excitable, thus better able to adjust to life as a pet. It should already be imprinted on humans.

Obviously, the best place from which to obtain your sugar glider will be a pet shop. Check with a number of pet shops to see what sort of service and price they are offering.

A seller should be able to tell you the age and sex of the pet. The housing conditions should be spacious and clean. There should be no indication of excess fecal matter in cages, or on perches (branches). Food and water pots should be clean and free of chips or cracks. The area surrounding the caging (floor, work surfaces) should be clean. The seller should supply you with the animal's feeding schedule; some also provide a health certificate if you request this. Its cost will be added to the cost of the pet. In some instances, you may receive a pedigree. The seller should be able to answer all your questions, even if you know the answers already because you have purchased this book. You want to deal with a knowledgeable and diligent person whom you can contact if any problems should arise. If you apply both patience and common sense to the buying process, you dramatically reduce the chance of your being dissatisfied.

WHAT AGE?

Sugar gliders are weaned and independent of their mother by about 16 weeks. This is the minimum age you should even consider. They are mature when about 9-10 months old, males usually a little older. When considering age, a youngster is definitely the better choice as a pet. You will see adults for sale, but these may not be "pet" tame. It is worth paying the extra to obtain your pet.

If a sugar glider has not been imprinted on humans by the time it's mature, it will never attain the same level of docility as one that has grown up around people. The only way you can establish if the pet is tame is by seeing it being handled, without problems, by the seller–then by yourself.

Age is not so much a factor for breeding stock, though young adults are obviously more desirable. Where adults are concerned you certainly want to know how old the individual(s) are.

PET OR BREEDER

Other than age, the difference between a pet or breeder, will be related to its appearance, and whether or not it is a proven breeder which is the most desirable characteristic.

The matter of appearance can be judged only by seeing many examples. When this is done, you will note that some have better markings and depth of color than others. Some will be a little larger than others, and some will have more profuse coats than others. Before purchasing breeding stock, you are advised to carefully read the chapter on breeding theory.

ASSESSING HEALTH

Before all else, the individual must be in the peak of health. Never mitigate any indication of poor health on the grounds it will get better with care. It may not. This would spoil the enjoyment you had expected from your sugar glider.

Males and females make equally good pets, barring the fact that a male will scent mark its territory.

As with any animal, what you see is not always what you get. What this means is that an individual may look healthy at the point of purchase, but could be incubating an illness that only manifests itself days later. This is why assessing the premises and conditions under which the pets are kept is as important as an examination of the individuals. If the conditions are good, the chances are equally as good that its health will be what it appears to be. When assessing health, start by trying to watch the pet move about in its cage. Do not get too close because this can prompt an unwell individual to move and look as though it's healthy. The glider should show no signs of impediment in its movements. If more than one individual is in the cage, are they all active?

It is possible that one may just be sleepy. But an individual that sits crouched in a corner and displays no interest in what is going on around it may be unwell. It is probably true if it remains in that position when you approach the cage. A very nervous individual will display a similar behavior–or may retreat quickly to its nestbox at your approach. Assuming all is well, select one that appeals to you. Have the seller take it out of the cage and handle it. If this goes well, the seller will normally allow you to handle the pet.

Commence your inspection with the head. The eyes should be round, bold and clear. The ears are erect. The fur is smooth and silky. It covers the entire body and tail. It should return to its lie when brushed against this. The anal region should be clean. There should be five digits on each foot. A missing digit is not any great handicap, but it's better if this is not the case. You can sex the individual by inspecting its abdomen. The male's scrotum (testicles) shows as a swelling about where your own belly button is found. This area is smooth on the female. The urinary tract in both sexes and the penis in males are near the anus. The marsupium of the female is normally only apparent when she is in breeding condition.

COST

Young proven breeders will be the most expensive. Pet stock will range in price based on its quality and what the local supply/demand situation is at the time. Both sexes make good pets, though the female does not scent mark her territory like the male. She may cost a little more, being more desirable on this account. Color mutations, when they appear, will initially command more money than 'normal' (wild coloration). They will then fall back in price based on the ease with which the mutation can be perpetuated.

In conclusion, it is stressed that you should acquire the pet's housing before you purchase the sugar glider(s).

FEEDING

The sugar glider is omnivorous in its dietary needs. This means it requires foods of both plant and animal origin. You cannot duplicate exactly the same items it would eat in the wild, but you can provide foods that have much the same range of constituents.

The feeding of any animal is not an exact science. It is more an art form that combines known nutritional knowledge with your ability to make observations of the appetite and health of your pet.

A FEEDING OVERVIEW

When you consider diet, this can be divided into a number of subjects. There is the important matter of what the animal needs with respect to the actual foods, and the role they play in body metabolism. However, what it needs and what it will actually eat may sometimes be in opposition. This situation is greatly influenced by the way in which its own parents were fed, and its diet in the period from weaning to when you obtained it.

There is then the matter of quantity. This will be influenced by the age of the pet, activity level, state of health, and breeding state. A bred female will obviously require more food than one which has no offspring to rear. The individual metabolism of each pet will not be the same. Some pets are called "easy keepers." They are

Protein, fruit, vegetables, and grain are the main components of a sugar glider's diet. It is important to feed your pet at the same time each day.

able to reach and maintain peak health on a diet and quantity that might not be adequate for another individual of the same size and weight. Always regard each sugar glider as an individual, separate from all others.

THE CONSTITUENTS OF FOOD

Based on the foods some beginners supply to their pets, and by the many questions I am asked

The survival diet is the very minimum in variety and quantity that enables the pet to live and stay basically healthy–assuming all other aspects of its management are excellent. This is not to say that such a diet is adequate either for a breeding animal, or one that is to achieve the maximum growth and vigor of its genetic potential. The constituents of each food item

A sugar glider will enjoy variety in its diet. Observe your pet at mealtime to determine which foods it favors.

concerning diets, it is clear some owners do not appreciate that foods vary considerably in their nutritional value. We should distinguish between these foods.

Distinction should also be made between a survival diet, and that which meets the full needs of peak health.

vary. Some foods may be especially rich in a given vitamin, or mineral. Others may lack these, but contain others that are equally as important.

Generally, foods of fruit and vegetable origin are high in vitamins, low in protein, fats, and carbohydrates. They are high in water content. Grain foods are high in carbohydrates, variable (but usually low) in proteins and fats, and low in water content. Their vitamin content is usually limited. Animal origin foods, such as meat, poultry, and invertebrates, are high in protein and fat, adequate to high in vitamin content, and low in carbohydrates. Proteins are made of amino acids. These are the building blocks from which muscle, brain, genes and blood are essentially created. Fats are important in giving foods their particular taste. They are also used to move other compounds around the body via the blood system. Fats provide insulation against the cold, a reserve supply of energy, and a buffer between the skin and bones.

Carbohydrates provide an inexpensive source of energy for day-to-day muscular activity. They provide needed bulk to the diet. Vitamins are essential to the immune system to help fight pathogens. They also enable many vital metabolic activities in body cells to be completed. Minerals, which are present in all foods, are essential to cell and bone structure. They greatly influence the movement of fluids (via the process known as osmosis) between the cells that make up the various parts of the body. Finally, water is essential to metabolism. The body of any animal is largely composed of water. It is lost via perspiration, respiration, urine, fecal matter and, in the case of

nursing females, via their milk. This loss must be replaced by the water content of the food, plus water consumed. This keeps the animal in water balance. The diet must reflect all of these needs. It must be carefully balanced so the risk of important ingredients being omitted is avoided. You can do this by ensuring you supply a range of food items containing all of the constituents discussed.

FOOD FORMS

Food can be supplied in various forms. It may be dry, semi-moist, moist (often called softfood), or live. It may be supplied in a natural form, or commercially prepared. It may be given as single items, mixes, or mashes. Ideally, you will supply some of each type. This will provide a diet that is well balanced between those items, such as dry foods, that have high concentrations of constituents, and those that have excellent water content.

We should not overlook another important aspect of food. Eating is not just a metabolic necessity. It has strong social and psychological influences that are sometimes negated when diets are commercially produced, or when restricted diets are supplied. The animal needs to be able to select from an assortment of items, each of which offers your pet the opportunity to satisfy its smelling, tasting and chewing needs. When this opportunity to be selective is denied, it may make the individual much more prone to stress.

WHEN AND HOW MUCH TO FEED

The sugar glider is a nocturnal animal. This will normally dictate its feeding times–in the early to mid-evening when it starts to become active. It can, however, have some dry foods left out to be taken at will during the day. If you wish, you may feed twice a day–early morning, and in the evening. The important thing is that the feeding time should be consistent. The pet will soon come to expect its meals at this time.

You can determine the quantity needed on a trial-and-error basis. This takes only a day or two to ascertain. The dietary needs of these pets will be in the range of 25-35% protein (meat, invertebrates) and 65-75% fruit, vegetable and grain. Growing youngsters and breeding females need the higher protein content. Non-breeding adults require a maintenance diet which will have the lower protein content. To establish quantity, prepare a mixture of items you feel will be sufficient. As a guide, start with one quarter cupful of mixed fruit/ vegetables, plus protein foods, per animal. See how much of this is eaten over a one-hour period. Of that left, some will be eaten later. By the time the next meal is due there will be either little, or nothing, left. If the former, you are feeding about the right quantity; if the latter, you should increase the amount slightly. If there is nothing left after the first hour, you are not giving enough. Clean water must be available at

As is true for other pets, drastic changes in diet should be avoided. Introduce new foods gradually, in small increments. When you first bring your sugar glider home, offer it the same diet that it is accustomed to for several days.

all times.

When the pet is first acquired, it is prudent to continue with its previous diet for a few days. This allows the pet to adjust to its new life without the extra strain of adjusting to an unfamiliar diet. Once the pet seems at ease and content, you can begin widening the diet—assuming this is deemed beneficial.

WIDENING THE DIET

Some breeders and pet shops feed only basic diets to their stock. This can create initial problems for you as you try to increase the pet's range of acceptable foods. Carefully note the order of preference for different items, and those which are rejected altogether.

When offering new items, withhold the most favored food. Replace it with one of a similar food value, that is, one of fruit, vegetable, or meat. If this is ignored over the first 30 or so minutes, you can supply the one it will eat. By this method you can steadily introduce your pet to a wide range of items, establishing a preference order for them. If the pet tends to gorge one or two favorite items, reduce the quantity of them a little. This will encourage it to take others in order to satiate its appetite. This is mentioned because favorite items are not always those from which it will derive the most nutritional benefit.

Bear in mind, the diet you are feeding to your sugar glider is artificial. The pet must eat a balanced diet as best as we can establish. If it gorges itself on a favored item it may reject another which is more wholesome. When a fruit or meat item is ignored, this may be because the pet is unfamiliar with it. You can persuade it to take such items by cutting them into very small pieces and mixing them with well-liked foods. In this way, the pet may come to acquire a taste for them. It may, subsequently, accept them as items in their own right.

As was stated earlier, feeding is as much an art form as a science. You must observe your sugar glider when it eats. You will learn a great deal from this about the foods and your pet. For example, if favored items are suddenly ignored this could indicate an impending problem–a mild illness. If a pet is ill it can often be tempted to eat an especially favored tidbit. A final comment with regard to feeding is that if you have two or more sugar gliders sharing the same accommodations, be aware that these pets, like all other animals, have a hierarchical order of superiority (a pecking order). This can be very evident at feeding times. If you're not alert, the individual(s) at the bottom of the order may not get their share of favored or important nutritional items.

If you notice this is the case, the way to overcome the situation is to provide two or more feeding stations as far apart as possible. Alternatively, feed one or more of the pets in their cage, the other outside of it.

SUGGESTED FOOD ITEMS

The following list of items is by no means exhaustive. It will give

exposure life. Anything left uneaten after a few hours should be removed before it sours. All foods should be stored in dark, dry, cool cupboards, or in refrigerators. In the latter case, be sure the food is thawed before it is fed to your pet. The list of fruits is

A healthy sugar glider will have a good appetite. Food can be offered in three forms: dry, semi-moist, and moist.

you a general guide to the various readily available foods. Never be afraid to experiment with other items. They will fall within one or another of the groups. Always ensure that foods are fresh. If you have any doubts, discard the item.

Likewise, if you have doubts as to the safety of an item—such as wild plants–play safe and ignore them.

Fruits, vegetables, and all moist or softfoods, have a limited

extensive and includes apple, apricot, banana, cantaloupe, cherry, date, fig, grape, melon, orange, peach, pear, persimmon, pineapple, plum, prune, raisin, and strawberry. Fresh fruits are better than canned. The sweeteners added to canned fruits will not be good for the teeth of your pet. The occasional canned fruit will not be a major problem as a treat.

The vitamin, mineral, and caloric values of these fruits

vary considerably, which is why a variety is the best policy. The various vegetables you can feed your pet are asparagus, bean, beet (including the top), broccoli, carrot, cauliflower, celery, chive, cress, lentil (dried), lettuce, dandelion, parsley, peas, potato (boiled), soybean, spinach, tomato, and turnip.

Some breeders attach great importance to lettuce, so it has been well promoted in articles. However, its vitamin E content is hardly impressive, while numerous other foods exceed it in iron, the two constituents that are often associated with it. In this author's opinion, lettuce, which has a water content in excess of 94%, is a food that offers very little nutritional benefit when compared to most other vegetables. Good seeds and nuts to provide would be almond, Brazil nut, cashew nut, canary seed, hazelnut, peanut (unsalted), millet, pine nut, rice (boiled) safflower, semolina, sunflower, sweetcorn, and tonic bird seed blocks.

Nuts, especially, are generally very rich in vitamin E. Sugar gliders are normally able to break through hard shells with surprising ease. If they have problems, break the nut for them. Various bird seeds can be supplied in a small dish, or added to a moist mash containing a range of foods. If you wish to increase the vitamin and general nutritional value of seeds, soak them for 24-36 hours in a shallow dish of water. Place this in a dark, dry cupboard. It will prompt the seeds to germinate, when little green shoots will appear. Rinse the seeds carefully under the faucet before feeding; this removes potential surface toxins.

Soaked seeds are readily digested. They are useful for young, or ailing pets. Once germinated they cannot be stored. Any not consumed must be discarded. Never feed any seeds whose shells are split and discharging a sticky sap–these will be toxic to your pet.

MEAT, INVERTEBRATES AND OTHER PROTEIN

Foods: Beef, beef extracts, canned dog or cat foods, crickets, cheese (these vary considerably in their protein and fat content), dry cat biscuits of various flavors, egg (boiled or raw, though the latter is messy), hamburger (cooked or raw), mealworms (but not maggots), poultry (cooked chicken is the most popular: remove the skin), sausage (type according to taste and familiarity), and white fish (boiled).

It is best to avoid meats that are too fatty. Do not gather invertebrates (worms, insects and their like) from your yard. These may contain the eggs of parasites. Obtain invertebrates from your pet store, or commercial breeders of them. You can supply 3-5 mealworms to each sugar glider every day, or every other day, alternating them with small slivers of meat or chicken–plus the fruit and vegetable part of the diet. Other items: milk, wholemeal bread, cookies, selected flower heads. Avoid candy. Honey and nectar are favored and natural food items for these pets. Be cautious with them during hot weather. Wasps may be attracted

any of the items discussed. Chop them up into very small pieces–be sure the mash is just moist, not sloppy. With this method, the pet is not able to be as selective over what it takes, so it may develop a taste for items it would ordinarily ignore.

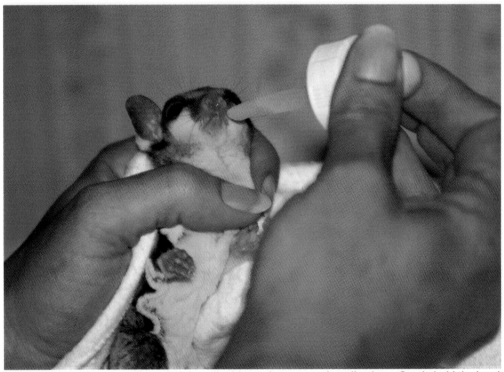

An eye dropper can be used to administer liquid supplements and medications. Gently hold the head upright so that the animal can swallow easily.

to them. Nectar can be obtained from your pet store and supplied in a small bird fountain feeder. Honey can be smeared on bread or fruit.

MASHES

You can make up a moist mash containing many items by using soaked bread crumbs, or porridge, as a base. To this can be added

SUPPLEMENTS

Vitamin and mineral supplements are very much in vogue these days, so a word of caution is appropriate. Lack of vitamins is known as vitaminosis and can be dangerous to good health. Its opposite, an excess of certain vitamins— hypervitaminosis—is no less dangerous. If your sugar glider

Fresh fruits and vegetables should not be left out for any great length of time, as they will spoil. Remove any that are uneaten after several hours. This is particularly important in warm weather.

eats a wide ranging diet that includes foods from each of the groups discussed, and exhibits good coat and health, supplements are not required. Do not supply them just for the sake of doing so. A supplement should be given only when a problem is detected or suspected. In such a case, discuss the matter with your veterinarian. The problem may have another source that will not be corrected with these supplements. If your newly obtained pet is eating only from a very limited range of foods, one of the commercial supplements may be beneficial while you widen the diet.

Dinner time for a hungry sugar glider. A good diet will be reflected in your pet's overall appearance.

OBESITY

If a pet does not get enough exercise, and is being fed excessive amounts of high protein, fatty, or stodgy foods, it may become obese. To avoid this situation, weigh your pet when it's obtained, then monitor its weight from time to time. If it needs to lose weight, this should be done carefully. First, withhold tidbits you know have no nutritional value. Reduce the quantity of fatty foods. Next, reduce the quantity of high protein foods, and those with high carbohydrate content.

This should be sufficient to bring the weight down, yet avoids the risk that important ingredients are being withheld from the diet. Do not expect dramatic weight loss within a week or two. It may take two or more months to achieve the desired weight. In conclusion, feeding should never be a mundane chore for you.

It is arguably the most important area of husbandry. The size, health, and general vigor of your sugar glider will be a direct reflection of its diet. Always try to make this something the pet looks forward to. Prepare a weekly menu containing some staple items, and items that are given rotationally.

Try to avoid feeding the pet and not watching its eating habits. You will learn a great deal about your pets just by the way they eat, and the items taken first. It is a very important part of their social well-being and worthy of regular observation.

BREEDING THEORY & STRATEGY

When you look at any outstanding example of a pet, you are seeing the result of two influences. One is the way it has been fed and reared–the environmental influence. The other is the genetic make-up of the individual. This gives the pet a very fixed potential of excellence. Management determines how much of this is achieved.

Clearly, if a sugar glider with great genetic potential is not cared for, its potential will never become apparent–though it will pass this to its offspring. Conversely, an individual with only modest genetic potential can look quite impressive if its owner has obtained its maximum potential by high standards of management. However, it will still be a moderate example. That is what it will pass to its offspring. In this chapter we will look at a range of topics that will be beneficial to you in a practical manner. Some understanding of the principles of heredity (genetics) is obligatory if you wish to maximize on the advice given. The theory will be explained using simple examples.

THE IMPORTANCE OF INITIAL STOCK

When starting a breeding program, the first advice is to obtain the best sugar gliders you can. There are no standards of excellence to compare against, so the following are points of importance.

1) Choose typical examples in respect of their size. This means you should see a number of individuals. Avoid keeping breeding stock that displays wide variation in size.
2) Be especially selective where the male is concerned. His importance on a mating-to-mating basis is more than that of the female. He is given greater status because he can more readily spread his genes through a population than can the female. She may have only 1-3 litters a year; he can sire many more.
3) By preference, obtain stock from a good line of sugar gliders backed up by accurate breeding records. But, if the best glider you see has no paperwork, it may still be valuable to your program. The reason for "may," rather than "will," is because it does not follow that a good-looking individual will pass these looks to its offspring. They may be a chance result of gene combinations.
4) By viewing many examples, you will form a mental image with regard to the quality of the fur, the color pattern, and its density of color. You want stock that shows dense silky fur. The lines of demarcation of colors should be as distinct as possible. The eye ring and striped pattern should be

complete, not broken. The colors should be bold, not vague and pale.

5) The stock should all display superb health and excellent temperament. These are very important considerations.

RECORD KEEPING

From the outset of your breeding program, do keep detailed records. These are discussed in the following chapter. Without them, you cannot hope to steadily improve the quality of your stock, or identify the source of problems should they arise.

THE PEDIGREE

You may or may not receive a pedigree with your sugar glider. It is better if you do. In its basic form, a pedigree is a list of an individual's ancestors. Without knowledge of their virtues and faults, it has no value to you as a breeder. It indicates line of descent, not quality or purity. However, a pedigree can still be very valuable.

It is not important that you have information on animals four or five generations back. Their contribution to the genes of the individual who bears the pedigree will be limited, at best. The exception to this is if certain of the ancestors appear a number of times–examples of line- or inbreeding. In this instance, there is a reasonable chance a number of their genes will have been passed to subsequent generations. The parent and grandparents are the two most important ancestors if

you are researching useful information. Bear in mind, regardless of how outstanding the parents are, if the individual is mediocre, its pedigree does not change this.

A pedigree is only as good as the individual that bears it.

OTHER CONSIDERATIONS

Be sure you have adequate facility to house the offspring you produce before you commence breeding. The better prepared you are in every way, the smoother your program will develop. Remember, it takes time to establish a good breeding program.

HOW FEATURES ARE INHERITED

The science of heredity is called genetics. Regardless of whether or not you understand the theory, you will be applying its principles the moment you pair one glider with another. By having an appreciation of how features are inherited, you will be better positioned to plan a breeding strategy that takes account of its benefits and drawbacks.

The unit of inheritance is called a gene. In every body and sex cell there are thousands of these microscopic units of coded information. They tell the cells how to develop. They are found in linear fashion along strands of tissue called chromosomes. The latter are in similar sized pairs, other than the sex pair. These are of different length. Some gene pairs have the power to control a feature by themselves. They are major genes.

Their effect is easily identified, being discontinuous. An example would be the albino. It is quite distinct from any other color form, and they from each other. Other features are controlled by the combined action of many genes; they are said to be polygenic. These features are continuous.

Continuous means that the features display a variation between two extremes. An example would be height or body length. Most features are of this type. When we talk of features, this includes all aspects of the individual, not just those that are visual. Resistance to disease, breeding vigor, temperament, motherhood, intelligence, and proneness to diseases and deformities are all subject to gene action, or are a direct result of it. When a pair of gliders mate, they can pass only one of their paired chromosomes and the genes on that chromosome to their offspring. In this manner the paired chromosome situation is restored at each generation.

The position of a gene on its chromosome is called its locus. At that same locus on its partner chromosome is another gene controlling the same feature. Two genes therefore determine the feature in a simple gene action situation, many pairs in a polygenic feature. If the paired genes are for the same expression in both parents, the offspring will have an identical genotype to its parents. This will create the same appearance, or expression. However, if the genes at each locus

are for different expressions, matters may change.

In a simplistic example, if we say gene **A** stands for good and **a** for bad, **AA** is the genotype for this feature (one **A** on each of the paired chromosomes): it is good. Such a parent can only pass an **A** gene to its offspring. If the other parent is **AA** it, too, can only pass an **A** gene. The same is true if both parents are **aa**. If, however, one parent is **AA** and the other is **aa**, the offspring can only have a genotype of **Aa**. What will they be like? The answer will be determined by the power of each gene to express itself when combined with its alternative form. This may be in the following ways.

1) If the genes have equal power, the feature will be somewhere between the expressions of each parent. This situation is normally seen in polygenic features. It is known as being additive. The extent to which additive genes determine a feature is the basis for expressing heritability. For example, size may have a high heritable value–possibly in the order of 70% or more. These features are the easiest for you to manipulate. Temperament has a high heritable value, though it is more difficult to assess–it is highly influenced by the environment (the way the animal is reared).

Litter size has a low heritable value, especially in animals that have only 1-3 babies per litter. Even in animals with large litter sizes, breeder selection for this trait will be less predictable than with other features.

2) If gene **A** has the greater power, gene **a** will not be apparent–but it will still be present. It has an equal chance of being passed to its offspring. Color, pattern, deformities, and mutations deemed desirable by breeders (which may not be from the animal's viewpoint) are usually of this type. They are non-additive. They may be modified by polygenes. For example, a major gene may control the white area of a glider, but polygenes (additive) will determine the shade of white from snow to almost cream or gray. The polygenes are therefore continuous.

3) Gene **A** may only be effective if another gene type at another locus is present—we will call this gene **B**. It may even require the presence of genes **B** and **C** before **A** becomes effective. This type of gene action is the most difficult of all to deal with. It assumes the breeder can identify the combination needed, which is rarely the case. This gene type of action is non-additive.

To complicate matters, even in simple additive features, it cannot be assumed that the proportions of the feature, for example in conformation, will remain the same. If the head represents 20% of the body at typical size it may, or not, do so as the size moves up or down. This will obviously affect the appearance of the individual. A final comment on gene actions is that some genes are linked to others. In such instances, as long as you require both features there's not a problem. But if intense selection for the one feature negatively intensifies the other feature, problems will arise. Sometimes linked features can be separated, sometimes they cannot. Fortunately, polygenic features are generally inherited independent of non-additive traits, such as color.

GENETIC TERMINOLOGY

So you have a better insight to aspects of breeding strategy, an understanding of a few common genetic terms will be useful. A dominant gene can express itself when in single or double dose. In the former case, it will suppress and mask the presence of a recessive gene at the same locus. It is denoted by use of a capital letter.

A recessive gene must be present in double dose before it can express itself. It is denoted by use of a lower case letter. Dominant and recessive genes at the same locus control the same feature. They are alternative possibilities at that locus. This is denoted by their using the same letter. For example, full color has the letter **C**. Its alternative is no color, or albino. This uses the letter **c**, which also indicates it's a recessive gene. A **CC** parent can pass only a **C** gene, a **cc** only a **c**. Their combination would produce **Cc**. Such an individual could pass either a **C** or a **c**–not both. The gene received from the other parent would determine the genotype and phenotype of the offspring.

The genotype is the genetic composition of a feature. This can only be documented accurately for mutational forms. In all other instances it can only be explained by theory based on many years of study. The phenotype is the physical outward expression (appearance) of a feature. The same phenotype may not result from the same genotype. For example, a **CC** genotype looks the same as a **Cc** because **C** is dominant to **c**. Such individuals will breed very differently, an important point to remember.

Homozygous means the same, or purebreeding, for a given genotype. **CC** and **cc** are both of this type. They can pass only one sort of gene. Heterozygous refers to different, or non purebreeding, for a given genotype. **Cc** is of this type. The individual could pass either a **C** or a **c** to its offspring. From the foregoing overview of inheritance, it can be seen that successful breeding involves the manipulation of genes that are themselves complex in the way they control features. It is generally assumed that desirable genes are best in the homozygous form. But this could be far from the truth; we do not know on a feature-to-feature basis.

Even without this consideration, a serious breeder's problems are immense. If **AABBCC** is the desirable state for each of three features, **aabbcc** being undesirable, how do we attain the former when we cannot express a polygenic feature in genetic formulae as we can with major mutational forms—such as albino, longhair, and their like? We have to do it based on a theoretical strategy, for better or worse. A genotype of **AaBbCc** (the average individual) can be passed to an offspring in eight combinations of these letters (**ABC**, **ABc**, **AbC**, **aBC**, and so on). The permutation of these with those of the other parent means there are 64 potential genotypes, 8 of which will be homozygous for each of their letters.

The chances of obtaining **AABBCC**, the ideal appearance, if this was not the starting genotype of each parent, will be exactly 1 in 64. Likewise, there will be the same chance of obtaining the worst example, **aabbcc.** Some will excel in one or two features, but be weak in others.

SELECTION–THE KEY TO SUCCESS

If we randomly mate the average individual, it is likely we will have a preponderance of stock that is average at each generation, give or take some on either side of this. There is always the possibility (1 in 64) that we could produce an outstanding animal–but equally one that is inferior.

To move the average in the direction we require, we must select continually in order to remove the inferior individuals from the breeding program. Breeding without selection will never improve the average quality of the stock. Selection requires a consistent method. Some

Male sugar gliders have several scent glands. The one in the middle of the head is the most obvious.

suggestions are given in the following chapter. We must also limit the potential genotypes from which we are breeding. If we do not do this, we risk undoing all that might have been achieved. For example, by careful selection from a "closed" gene pool, we have attained **AABBCc** stock. We have removed all **a** and **b** genes. Those features are superb. We obtain at random an individual that looks quite nice. But are **A** and **B** homozygous? If not, we will immediately introduce **a** and **b** genes to the program. We will be back where we started, maybe many generations earlier.

Conversely, if we started with **AaBbcc** stock, we can reach an ideal state in **A** and **B** by judicious selection. But we can never attain **CC** or even **Cc** because the **C** gene was never there at the outset. Only well into the program might this become apparent. Here we are confronted with the advantages and disadvantages of the breeding strategy we have used. We will review them here.

RANDOM BREEDING

This is probably the most common form of breeding. Convenience is often a major factor, rather than what is likely to be achieved. By definition, random implies that some inbreeding may take place.

Random breeding does minimize the problems that could come with inbreeding. Rarely can it produce an outstanding individual. Such an example rarely breeds to its own excellence, often being very disappointing. It is the 1 in 64 chance. In reality, assuming many more than just three genes (as in our example), it is a 1 in many thousands chance. Unfortunately, when such an individual appears, it is often used extensively in breeding programs. By the time its lack of breeding worth is apparent, it has spread many of its unwanted genes in its breeder's, and other's, stock.

Random breeding will include matings such as like to like and compensatory matings. In the former instance the assumption is that if two individuals look similar, they will produce offspring of the same type. This may be the case where inbred individuals are concerned, but not necessarily so with unrelated stock. The reason is that the gene combination that gives two individuals similar looks may not be the same, particularly if the pair are of differing sizes. Even where the results are good, there is probably little homozygosity. Using these individuals in order to improve faults in other stock will be less predictable than using inbred or linebred stock.

Compensatory matings are when an individual is paired to another in order to remedy an undesirable feature. This is an ongoing situation in a breeding program. Doing this with conformation, you should always use an example that excels in the feature, but not be excessive. For example, if snout length is too short, you pair to one with ideal length, not a long-snouted example. The latter would tend to increase heterozygosity for this feature.

INBREEDING & LINEBREEDING

These two strategies are actually the same, linebreeding being a less intense form of inbreeding. The latter is often misunderstood by those with no genetic knowledge. It does not of itself create anomalies as is often thought. It merely increases the chances that problem genes in the stock will manifest themselves. If undesirable genes do not exist in two individuals, no amount of inbreeding can create them.

Inbreeding, combined with rigorous selection, is the means by which desirable features are made homozygous. Practiced over many generations, inbreeding can result in breeding depression, and other problems. The average breeder is unlikely to conduct very close matings for the number of generations likely to bring this about. The method should increase the homozygosity of possible unwanted features, the more so if they are linked to features deemed desirable. The other problem with intense inbreeding is that it does limit your options.

Once you have attained the maximum potential for the genes you are working with, you must introduce fresh genes if the ones you have are not achieving the desired standard. In doing this, you take the risk of regression in all that your inbreeding has achieved. The introduced individual may be heterozygous for those features in which you have attained homozygosity, even though it looks excellent. Conducting inbreeding at a less intense level (called linebreeding), you work with a wider gene pool that is not as limiting. It will probably take longer to achieve your objectives, but it is the safer course taking all factors into consideration.

It offers many of the advantages of both random matings and close inbreeding, while avoiding many of their inherent problems. You are working with a "closed" pool of genes, but one that provides a good degree of flexibility. The basis of line breeding is that your matings are at cousin or further removed level, with maybe the occasional sibling matings (brother/sister) or parent/ offspring to intensify wanted features. The object of the strategy is to increase the possibility that the desirable genes of a given individual are passed to subsequent generations.

If that individual was mated to a number of other relatives of an individual in successive generations, it is reasonable to assume this will be the case (but the undesirable genes may also have increased). With an appreciation of the value of understanding gene actions as presented in this chapter, you can consider the importance of such combinations in your breeding endeavors. You will gain immensely from seeking out more detailed books. They will not be specific to sugar gliders, but this doesn't matter. The principles of heredity, on which the science is based, apply to all animals.

PRACTICAL BREEDING

The first comment with regard to breeding these pets is that it should not be done merely to perpetuate the species. The only things this achieves are to generally reduce the standard of quality in the population as a whole, and to bring down prices. The latter has both beneficial and negative effects. Clearly, it makes these pets more affordable–a benefit–but in the process increases the number of casual and unplanned breedings–a negative. Many pets are then bred by owners whose knowledge is very limited.

PREPARING FOR BREEDING

Your first thoughts should be directed at planning breeding operations, the extra housing needed, obtaining quality stock, preparing records, and deciding on the sort of breeding strategy you wish to pursue. Theoretical considerations, and some aspects of stock purchase, have been discussed in the previous chapter. Here we can consider the records, the actual breeding process, and various methods of selection you can use in order to retain the best offspring for future breeding.

PREPARE RECORD BOOKS

You cannot maintain a serious breeding program without keeping records. The more detailed they are, the more valuable they will be in the long term. However, it is better you have simple maintained records, than excessive paperwork that is not kept up to date. Records can be kept in many ways. The following are some suggestions.

1) **Individual Records.** This will indicate the name, number, sex, age, and source of the glider. Ideally, you will have a good photograph attached to this. Alternatively, or additionally, make a master sketch (skin plan) and have photocopies prepared. You can then record the full pattern markings of each individual. The record can also indicate who the glider was mated to, the result in terms of offspring numbers, sexes, health state, survival rate, and ID number each offspring retained. Health and other notes can be kept on the record, or placed on separate documents.

2) **Breeding records.** These can be of two types. One would be accumulative. It indicates which individuals were paired, when offspring were due, when they were actually born, their sex, color pattern (if appropriate), and any pre-weaning problems encountered. It might also show to whom each youngster was sold. The alternative record would be individual to each female, which would allow you to review her full breeding record more readily.

3) **Pedigrees.** These can be of 2-5 generation type. They are read horizontally, left to right. The sire and his ancestors are placed in the top half of the pedigree, the dam the lower half. The pedigree should indicate the date of birth, sex, color, ID number of the bearer, and the breeder's name and address. Against the actual ancestors it is useful to indicate ID numbers, and color if these are not normal (wild type), for example, albino, or whatever mutations may develop in these pets. Any special notes on individuals should be placed on the rear of the pedigree. You can easily design and have printed your own pedigree, or you can purchase blanks as used for dogs, cats and other pedigreed pets.

THE INITIAL STOCK

Assuming you commence with a low-key program, it is suggested you purchase a single breeding pair. These will be related, but not too closely. If you wish to start with two females, it would be prudent to obtain the second one from a different source to increase chances so that the females are unrelated. This gives you two breeding lines that will be related via the single male. Later, you can introduce an unrelated second male if you need to widen your genetic pool. This should provide a nucleus on which you can build for some generations without the need to introduce "unknown" genes via other stock.

BREEDING METHOD

Sugar gliders can, in theory, be bred in three ways.

1) A male and female can be housed together to produce and rear the litter. This is the most appropriate method for the beginner, and well used by established breeders. The male makes little contribution to the rearing process, but his presence is very natural for this species. His parental contribution when the family is in the nestbox may be greater than is generally realized.

2) A male can be housed with two or more females to breed as a colony. This is a popular method, though having more than two females in one unit requires a large space, with more than one feeding station. It is essential that the male be selected with great care in respect to his quality.

3) The females can be caged individually and exposed to the male solely for mating purposes. This would require a 30-day period. A mating would have to be assumed in the absence of actually seeing it. The drawback is that sugar gliders are social animals. Keeping one of either sex alone purely for breeding denies the individual the opportunity to live as it would in the wild. It will increase the likelihood of stress. It is not recommended as normal policy.

BREEDING CONDITION

This term refers to the general health state and fitness of each of the pair to be mated. It is especially appropriate to the female since it is she, and her babies, that will be affected if her condition is less than superb. However, an unfit male may have mating problems, or his contribution may result in one baby rather than two due to his temporary lack of fecundity. Never mate any animal that is unwell, recovering from an illness, or is under- or overweight. Some weeks before a mating, it is wise to worm the female. Double check there are no signs of mites or other ectoparasites in the housing. Pay special attention to the nestbox.

INTRODUCING STOCK

If you breed on a colony basis, the females should be introduced to each other at the same time. They will form their own hierarchy with less squabbling than if one is added to an existing pair, or a second to a cage already occupied, when the newcomer could be savagely attacked. The male is added only when the females are compatible with each other. He will certainly be harassed initially until he exerts his male dominance over the females.

BREEDING FACTS

Sexual Maturity: In the female this is achieved at the age of about 8-10 months, maybe sooner. It is somewhat later in the male, usually early in his second year.

The species is polyestrus, meaning the female has a number of breeding cycles during the year. The cycles last about 29 days. During this period there is a natural curve in respect of the female's willingness to be mated. Exactly when it peaks does not appear to have been documented. Mating will usually occur during the evening.

Gestation: This is the time from fertilization of the female's ova by a sperm, and the birth of the offspring. It is about 16 days.

Litter Size & Frequency: Normally, 1-2 babies, but there may rarely be 3. In the wild a female would have one or two litters per year. Under controlled domestic conditions, it is possible to obtain four litters. This is not recommended if you wish to allow the female to return to full physical condition between litters. To avoid this situation requires that either the male be removed from the family unit when a female has had 2-3 litters, or more commonly, that a female which has had 3 litters in a short period be removed from the unit for a period of rest with other non-breeding females.

Intense breeding can only reduce a female's vigor. It may adversely affect her long-term breeding life. It is often practiced when a hobby is new. This is why careful selection of vigorous and healthy initial breeding stock is so important.

Transfer to the Nipple: Once the baby is born, it will crawl from the vaginal opening to its mother's marsupium to take hold of a nipple. This immediately swells in its mouth so the youngster is firmly secured. The mother does not assist in this transfer, but licks the fur it has crawled over to remove birthing fluids.

The youngster will stay attached to the nipple for a variable number of days, up to about 40, after which it will remain in the pouch for another 30 days give or take a day or two. By the time it leaves the pouch, it is fully furred, its eyes open.

Leave the Pouch: When about 70 days old the infant will first leave the pouch–for progressively longer periods as the days go by. It will cling to its mother's underbelly at first, but will soon clamber on her back, indeed any part of her body if startled, in order to be transported.

Weaning: The young sugar glider is weaned from its mother's milk when about 105 or so days of age (15 weeks). The process actually commences as soon as the infant starts to sample foods. From this point onwards it steadily eats a greater amount, and a wider range of items, until it is independent. If left with her it will continue to suckle for a variable period. You are not advised to leave the youngsters in the company of a male for too long once they are independent. The weeks pass quickly. If the female reaches sexual maturity early, she will be mated, which may not be desirable.

SOCIALIZATION

Once the youngsters start to leave the pouch they should be gently handled on a regular basis. This bonds them to humans, making them better, and more desirable, pets. It is absolutely essential that they are fully independent of their mother before being transferred to new homes. Some may require one or more extra weeks with her than others. Do not apply fixed limits to when a baby should be independent–treat each as an individual case in its own right.

BREEDING PROBLEMS

There are no special breeding problems related to these pets at this time, other than any that might arise with any mammal. This having been said, it has been noted that some offspring, generally domestically bred and under one year of age, have become weakened, paralytic in the rear legs, and have died in a number of instances. Some have died suddenly without any outward signs of ill health.

The suspected causes are a deficiency in vitamin E/selenium, or a deficiency in the balance of calcium, phosphorus, and vitamin D. The latter, based on information supplied to me by Laura Lermayer, a noted breeder, seems to be the most likely. To reduce the risk of such a problem, you are advised to supply a calcium vitamin D supplement to females prior to breeding them, and throughout the nursing period.

If kept on a colony system, the supplement should be sprinkled

The sugar glider has five digits on each foot. All of them are clawed, except for the inner digits on the hind feet.

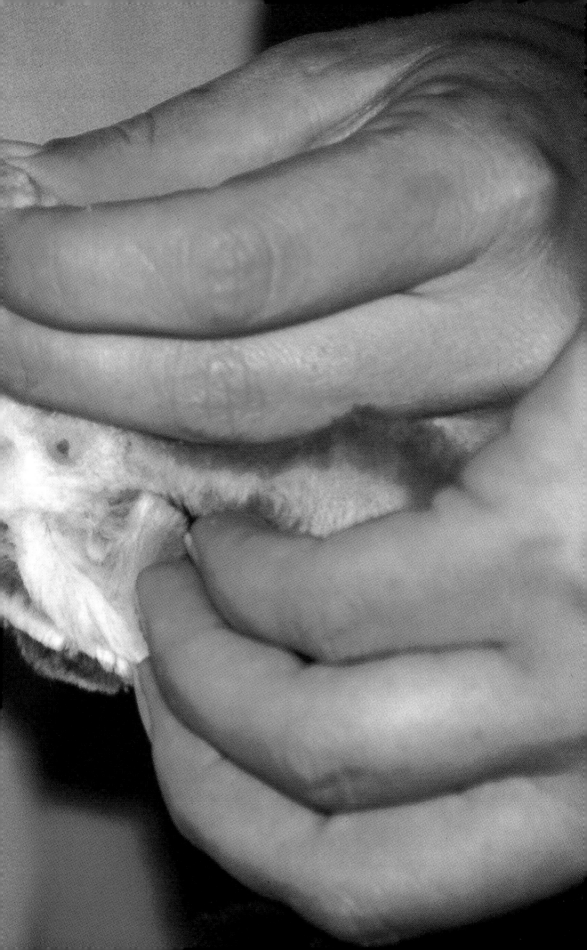

onto food items that all of the colony will get their fair share of. This could be important. It is also important that if this problem is seen in your pets, you should discuss the matter with your vet immediately. Excess calcium and vitamin D can themselves create problems, so professional advice is recommended.

METHODS OF SELECTION

Having produced your first litter, thoughts should be directed to the methods open to you for grading these. You will want to retain the best for onward breeding. The average breeder will normally make this selection in the weeks prior to weaning based on an inspection of the stock in absence of any documented criteria.

Wise breeders will carefully list the features they are seeking to maintain or improve. This way they are less likely to be carried away by a single feature that looks great, but which, in the overall needs of the stock, is really not that important. The success of selection methods can only ever be as good as the person making them, the way the system is structured, and the heritability of the feature being selected. Other than for color or pattern markings, you will be normally selecting for polygenic features, which are probably controlled in a simple additive manner. There are three basic methods from which to choose, plus an alternative strategy.

TANDEM SELECTION

With this method you select a feature that you wish to improve. You retain only those individuals that are superior to their parents for this. Once satisfied with progress, you select another feature, and so on. The method is used successfully by some breeders. It can result in dramatic improvement of a feature but has sufficient drawbacks to make it the least recommended method. It assumes there is no negative correlation between the features being selected. If there is, as one is improved, the others may regress. It also assumes that a feature is so poor that it is worthy of attention in isolation of all other features. This is unlikely in such a new pet where the general standard is reasonably constant when compared to pets established for many years.

INDEPENDENT CULLING (IC)

With this method you list the features you consider important, then grade them by letter or points based on your minimum acceptable standards. Only individuals that reach the minimums for each feature are retained. The method has the advantage, unlike tandem selection, of embracing multiple features. Progress is determined on a collective basis. What you must take into account is that the grading of each feature should bear some relationship to its importance. Do not apply the same minimum high standards to a feature that may not be as valuable as another.

For example, you would not wish to dismiss an individual because it failed on a minor pattern marking, when its temperament or general confirmation was outstanding. This so, pattern marking requirement would be given a lower minimum standard, temperament a high one. In general, the more features you select from the better.

However, this places greater importance on your ability to weight the values accurately. If not, you increase the possibility of individuals being dismissed because they failed on a triviality. Initially, you may make an error in the grading standards. Only after applying them will this become evident if you see an excellent individual being dismissed. Some fine tuning to the method may be needed based on its practical application.

Always remember that any selection should be based on retaining individuals that are superior to the average for a given feature. There is no gain if you retain only those which have few faults, but no great virtues.

TOTAL SCORE (INDEX SELECTION)

With this method each feature is listed and marked out of ten, or whatever figure. The retained stock is determined on the basis of a given minimum acceptable score. This has the advantage that an individual will not be dismissed on a trivial feature. It is the total score of all qualities that determines its importance.

The negative is that the method, as described, assumes each of the features are of equal value, which is rarely the case. You can improve it somewhat by allocating more points to important features than to minor ones. The problem here is that you are judging against a variable grading, rather than one which is consistent. This can be overcome by applying a coefficient to each, thus allowing the features to be assessed against a constant figure. For example, you grade each feature out of ten, but multiply this by its coefficient, which is variable based on the importance of the feature. Health may be given 5, temperament 4, confirmation 3, color 2, size, 2, tail length 1, and so on.

If health obtained 7 out of ten this would be multiplied by 5 to yield 35 points. If color received 8 out of ten this would be multiplied by 2 to yield 16. Once again, retention is based on a minimum required total score. In this variation it is imperative that the coefficients are well balanced. It ensures that major features are always given a greater opportunity to score higher than trivial features. As features are improved, or regress, their coefficient is adjusted to take account of present needs.

PROGENY TESTING METHOD

This method is quite different from the previous three. Here, you assess an individual based on its proven breeding performance, rather than on an estimated value that is unproven from a breeding perspective. It can be used in conjunction with one of the previous methods. For example, if an individual has been retained, it is hoped its features will be passed to its offspring–which they may not be. By evaluation on a litter-by-litter basis, you can establish which adults are passing on their traits, or certain of these. You use the combined litter evaluations to decide which of the parents are retained.

Bear in mind that an apparent excellent standard of performance by a male will as equally reflect the performance of the females he is mated to. Breeders often overrate males because they have underrated the value of the females. They may be of a good standard and have consistently masked the male's lack of actual breeding worth. From the methods discussed you will appreciate that a documented selection method will benefit you enormously. It enables you to track performance over any given number of generations, rather than from your memory. The latter is a very unreliable tool to use in a breeding program.

In general, whatever method is used should be applied consistently in time terms. Assessment of stock should be made at given ages. Do not judge offspring of one litter at three

Always check with a veterinarian before giving your pet any dietary supplement.

months and another at two months. In reality, it is beneficial to make selections as a result of two or three assessments over a given period. This will highlight

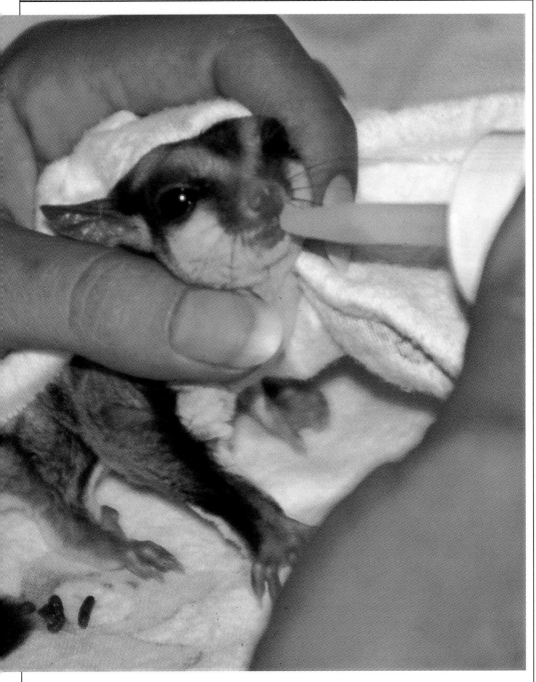

which features tend to change the most within a time frame, and which are reasonably predictable based on an assessment at any given age. It is stressed that health and temperament should always outweigh any other consideration. They are the cornerstones on which all other features should be developed.

HEALTH CARE

Maintaining excellent health in your sugar glider is achieved by sound husbandry techniques. Husbandry covers a range of topics.

1) Nutrition
2) Hygiene
3) Stress
4) Recognizing ill health
5) Reacting to ill health
6) Quarantine

Additionally, it can be useful to have some knowledge of various pathogens (disease causing organisms) and their vectors (the organisms that transfer the pathogens to your pet). This is by no means essential. Indeed, it can be a hindrance. The saying that a little knowledge is a dangerous thing is often true. It can prompt owners to attempt diagnosis and treatments that are wildly inaccurate. They could make matters worse. You are advised not to attempt this with your sugar glider. Leave health treatments to vets. Your knowledge is best directed at husbandry techniques that reduce the possibility of the pet becoming ill in the first place, rather than taking drastic steps in the event of a problem.

In most instances, illness follows some breakdown in husbandry technique. When this happens, owners tend to seek a quick and simple solution to what may be a complex series of events. They may seek a diagnosis based on a comment such as "he doesn't eat a lot of food," "she is scratching a lot," "he seems very lethargic," "his eyes are running," "she is vomiting," and others equally as vague from a diagnostic standpoint. There are a limited number of ways your pet can display signs of ill health, but there are thousands of pathogens and hundreds of illnesses. Only by methodical diagnosis, often involving microscopy of fecal and blood samples, can treatment be prescribed for any but the most obvious of problems. These would include external parasites, wounds, and their like.

NUTRITION

An individual will only be as healthy as its diet allows. If the diet lacks any needed constituents, the pet's susceptibility to problems increases in direct ratio to the number of nutritional deficiencies. Never allow the diet to become a mundane chore. Always observe each sugar glider to see what it eats, and its level of enthusiasm for given items. You are referred to the chapter on Practical Breeding for special problems related to a lack of calcium, phosphorus, vitamins D, E, and selenium.

HYGIENE

Although incorrect nutrition is the prime cause of many health problems, lack of hygiene rates higher where most diseases are concerned. It spans a very extensive range. It is so easy to leave for another day, or week, what should have been done daily or weekly. Food and water dishes must be cleaned and replenished daily. Surface cleaning of fecal matter should be a daily chore. The entire accommodation should be cleaned weekly, all floor covering being replaced. Stripped bark must be replaced, all other perches thoroughly cleaned. Cage bars and nestboxes should also be cleaned weekly. Removed debris should be disposed of at the time, not left in the same room as the caging. Cracked or chipped vessels should be discarded/replaced.

It is preferable (by numbering) to ensure food and water pots are returned to the same cage after cleansing. Always wash your hands before and after cleaning chores are completed, and before and after handling your pets. If a pet is ill it is wise to handle it with surgical gloves to reduce the risk of transferring pathogens from one pet to another via your hands. Avoid visiting pet shops, or friends with pets, if yours is unwell. You may transfer the problem to them via your clothing.

Purchase pet products only from clean stores. Be sure to store all foods in dark, cool cupboards or refrigerators, depending on their food type (dry or moist). Never risk feeding items that look and smell other than fresh.

Breeders must ensure there is ample ventilation in their stock room. Pathogens can easily build up to dangerous levels in the air.

During humid periods this is especially so, as they are encased in capsules of moisture that periodically empty as the humidity level drops.

STRESS

Stress is best defined as a subconscious condition that negatively affects the immune system. It also prompts anomalous behavior patterns that are of themselves deleterious to good health. It is generally thought the condition is created when an individual cannot react to its environment in the way it would in the wild. The more unnatural the environment, the greater the risk, and degree, of stress. The more natural the behavior pattern being suppressed, the greater the stress.

A problem with the condition is that it is not readily identified. Nor does it affect individuals to the same degree. What might stress one pet may not another, the reaction reflecting the individual's breeding (genotype) and rearing. Prime stressors are lack of housing space, incorrect diet (in respect to constituents and their presented form), lack of climbing facilities, overcrowding, habitual bullying where the bullied cannot retreat to a safe distance, lack of nestbox hygiene, excess and sudden noises (electrical appliances, engines), excess disturbances (children overhandling pets that are resting or sleeping, lights suddenly going on or off), lack of correct heat and cooling, irregular and sudden temperature fluctuations, and close proximity to things that might frighten the sugar glider (dogs and cats trying to paw at the caging, or similar intimidating events).

The effects of stress are wide-ranging. It should first be said that their clinical signs could be the result of other causes. These must be considered first when trying to determine if stress may be the problem.

1) Cage pacing. Usually indicates lack of space.

2) Coprophagia (eating fecal matter) and similar syndromes, such as fur biting (trichophagia), and wood or shavings chewing (lignophagia). These can be the result of a needed ingredient, usually a mineral, missing from the diet. More often, they indicate stress created by boredom or confined unclean conditions.

3) Self-inflicted wounds indicate a dietary deficiency, or boredom stemming from confinement and lack of things to do, such as climbing, and jumping. They often occur in single pets that become neglected after an initial high interest from their owners.

4) Hyperphagia (overeating) and polydipsia (excess drinking). The former may result from poor nutrition when the animal was young, or from incorrect dieting. It may also result from boredom. The pet gobbles its food ravenously, often not masticating it in the process.

A well-balanced diet can help to prevent health problems.

Intestinal problems then arise. Excessive drinking may result from close confinement and boredom. The excess intake can create metabolic problems, and those related to osmo-regulation of liquids between cells. It may arise from the syndrome of licking at the spout of an inverted water bottle. Although you can limit the amount of water supplied, this is not good husbandry. It is better to correct the causal problem.

5) Cannibalism. This problem is the result of inadequate diet and/or confined space, or overstocking of the space. The latter may be aggravated if it is unclean. It should be added that poor mothering instincts are genetic, but cannibalism is usually environmental. The stressed mother's state may prompt her to abandon or kill her babies for what may be the slightest provocation. She is at her limits of coping. It needs little extra mental pressure for her to turn on her offspring.

The foregoing are some of the more well-known causes and effects of stress. There are others, aggression and nervousness being obvious examples, but those are more likely to arise from the way the pet is treated. In most instances, once the stressor is removed, the problem stops.

In others, the anomaly may become a part of the individual's behavior pattern—it has become a habit. This situation is more difficult to overcome. One way of doing so is to relocate the pet's accommodations. The change in environment may help. Better still, replace and improve the housing with something altogether better.

RECOGNIZING ILL HEALTH

You have two ways in which to determine when your pet is unwell. One is by its behavior, the other by physical signs. Sometimes both will be seen. If only one is the case, it will normally be behavioral. This places great importance on your ability to recognize behavior changes. These can only be evaluated if you devote a good amount of time observing and interacting with your pet.

Behavior Changes

Eating & Drinking: Your pet will normally eat in a predictable manner. It may be dainty, average, or rather greedy. It will usually select from the foods offered in a predictable manner, eating its favorites first. It will usually consume a given amount during a given period of time. There will also be a similar pattern of drinking. Any changes from this pattern may indicate the onset of a problem.

If your pet suddenly starts to drink excessively this certainly would indicate something is amiss. Naturally, during warmer or colder weather, food consumption may rise or fall a little. During warm weather your pet may eat rather less, and drink somewhat more, than normal.

Likewise, if the diet is essentially of dry foods it will drink more than if it is subsequently given more moist foods. Sudden disinterest in food, especially if favored tidbits are offered, is very indicative of a problem, the more so if it persists longer than 24 hours.

Activity Level: Animals establish their own patterns of activity level just as you do. Sudden changes in these should be regarded as abnormal, unless you can justify them. For example, if a pet suddenly starts to spend far more than its normal time in its nestbox, this is cause for concern.

If the pet is seen crouching in a corner of the cage when it would not normally do this, you can suspect a problem. If it is very lethargic when normally it would be active, or if it shows disinterest in its relationship with you, or its companions, these are negative signs. If it makes sudden erratic dashes about the cage, or if it has problems in retaining its balance, a problem can be suspected. If your pet has an abnormally active period because you are able to spend more time than normal with it, you can expect it to sleep a little longer, be less active the next day, and maybe eat more than normal.

Physical Signs

Physical signs may be any of the following. If more than one is displayed this indicates a regressing situation. Weeping, swollen or sunken eyes, swollen or runny nostrils, coughing, vomiting, wheezy or labored breathing, diarrhea (especially if this is blood-streaked), constipation, excess scratching or biting at the fur, difficulty in eating, swellings of any kind (small or over a larger area, such as the abdomen), abrasions and cuts, bald areas of fur, dry looking fur with a flaky appearance, difficulty in moving, or grasping food or perches, weight loss and emaciation.

REACTING TO ILL HEALTH

Always do something once you have reason to suspect your pet is unwell. All animals, like humans, have their good and bad days. However, at the least, make a note of the time and day you observe abnormal behavior. From this point onwards your reaction should be governed by the progress of the problem, if there is one. Increase the number of observations. You should also inspect the pet carefully for any physical signs of a potential problem. Once a sign is evident, the nature and severity of this will dictate matters. Slight weeping of the eyes or nose may indicate a minor chill. Slight diarrhea could be the result of a minor tummy upset caused by a chill, or reaction to a food item.

These conditions should clear up within 24 hours. If they persist, contact your vet.

Scratching suggests external parasites or internal worms. Treatment is via a proprietary medicine from your vet. Excessive vomiting is the result of an internal problem–consult your vet. Breathing difficulties indicate an infection of the respiratory tract. This must be diagnosed by your vet. Abdominal swellings will be related to problems of the gastro-intestinal tract. There may be a blockage. This must be diagnosed and treated promptly. It could be fatal if left unattended for even a short period. Constipation also indicates an intestinal restriction. Small swellings could be the result of insect or arachnid (spider) bites, local infection caused by an object, bruising, or a tumor, or an internal problem.

Abrasions and sores are the result of surface irritants (bites, scratches), fungal infection (ringworm), or the outward signs of an internal disease or condition. In all of these instances you should isolate the pet. Makes notes on the clinical or behavioral signs. Detail when you first noted the problem, how quickly things have deteriorated, and in what ways. You should at this time completely review your husbandry practices to see if the problem is related to lack of hygiene, inadequate or stale foods, or possible contamination of these by mice or other vectors.

Inspect the feet periodically for any signs of injury, e.g., as might be caused by sharp cage wire.

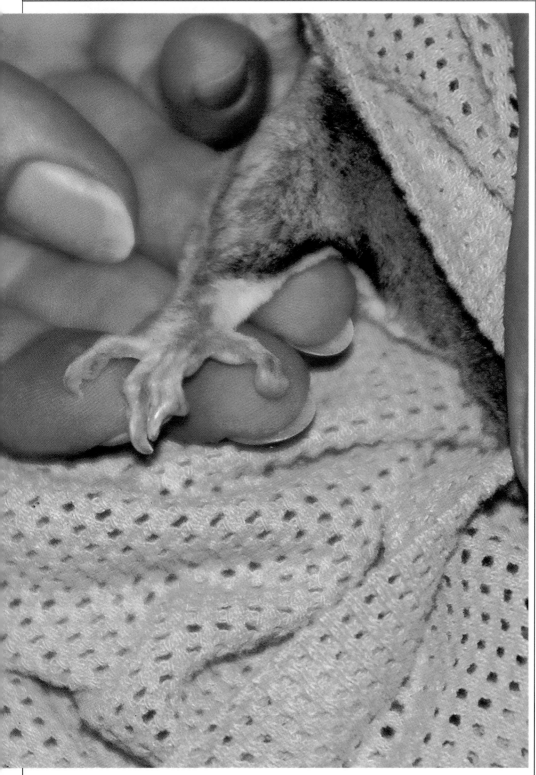

This information may be helpful to your vet. Now call the vet. The longer you delay, the more time you give the condition or disease to get worse and make treatment more difficult (and costly).

You should automatically, and thoroughly, clean the housing of any ill pet. Try to gather some samples of the fecal matter in a sealed plastic tube or pick them up via the fingers of a surgical glove and turn this inside out. Your vet will need these for analysis, such as egg counts for worms. Destroy all bedding. Clean nestboxes with household bleach, formaldehyde, glutaraldehyde, or such as recommended by your vet. Doing so will not only destroy bacteria and viruses, but also fungal spores (not all disinfectants will do this). Rinse clean to remove residual chemicals.

When confronted with a situation where you cannot immediately take the pet to a vet, try to increase the temperature of its accommodation a few degrees. Do this so that the pet can retreat to a cooler part of the cage if it becomes distressed by the heat. The use of a dull emitter infrared lamp is excellent for providing localized heat without the drawback of high light intensity. The latter will stress an unwell animal that wishes to sleep.

If diarrhea is evident, withhold softfoods (high moisture), but not water, for 24 hours. Where wounds are apparent, gently clean them with a mild non-irritant solution of hydrogen peroxide or antiseptic lotion that you can obtain from your vet.

QUARANTINE

The potential breeder should make every effort to provide some caging away from the main stock. This enables newly acquired individuals to be observed for any indication of health problems before they come into contact with the main stock. The suggested isolation period is 14-21 days. This should allow any incubating diseases to manifest themselves. During this period the new addition has the opportunity to become exposed to localized bacteria at a low level. This is especially important if the individual has been transported from a different region.

During the quarantine period you can monitor, and slowly adjust, feeding regimens and schedules to that used on the main stock. You should carefully examine new arrivals for signs of external parasites. A hand lens is useful. It would also be prudent for your vet to conduct a fecal analysis for worms. Once the individual is moved to the main stock room, its isolation cage should be very thoroughly sanitized using an appropriate chemical from your vet.

TREATMENTS

The range of modern drugs available today is extensive. Some are broad spectrum, meaning they are effective over a wide range of pathogens; others are more selective, or even species specific.

Most have a limited shelf life once exposed to the atmosphere.

For these reasons you should never use a medicine unless you are very sure of its effect, dosage, dangers, and shelf life. Never assume that if a little is beneficial, a lot will be even better. This could be dangerous, or even lethal. Most effective medicines are potentially toxic beyond a given dose. If they prove ineffective within a stated period of time, they should be discontinued and a vet consulted.

Some medicines can be given concurrently, others cannot. They contain similar compounds that might make their combination toxic.

Bear all of these facts in mind before seeking advice from any non-qualified person. It is also stressed that trying to obtain diagnosis and treatment advice from a breeder over the telephone is not conducive to good husbandry. A sick sugar glider needs to be professionally inspected for the best chance of correct treatment.

Nails must be trimmed frequently. This can be accomplished by wrapping the sugar glider in open-mesh fabric. Clip only the white portion of the nail—never the pink area.

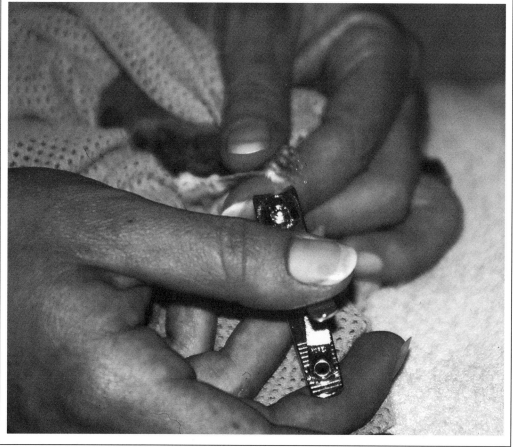

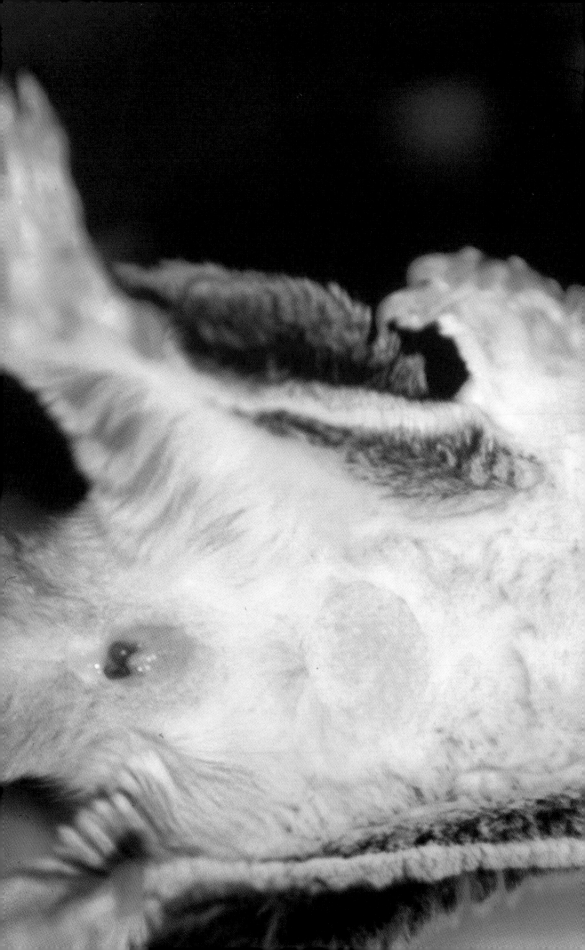

The sugar glider's soft fur can be a hiding place for parasites, so check your pet regularly.

REGULATIONS AFFECTING SUGAR GLIDERS

Although many pet owners are not always aware of it, there are regulations that apply to the keeping of any pet animal, be it a bird, rabbit, cat, or dog. In the case of long-established pets these normally present no problems. This is not so with the new generation of exotic animals.

It is by no means always easy to establish what the laws are for these exotic pets, of which the sugar glider is one. The following text is not definitive, but will serve as a general guide to potential owners. It answers some of the questions such owners often ask when they find out that wanting one of these pets, and legally being able to keep one, are separate issues. The laws are controlled by federal, state, and local agencies.

Each of these, and there are many of them, issue their own regulations. If you do not abide by these laws your pet may be confiscated. You may be fined, even imprisoned. To claim ignorance of the law does not excuse your being subject to it.

Unfortunately, where exotic pets are concerned, it can be far from easy to establish exactly what laws you must comply with in your locality. For this reason, many exotic pet owners across the United States keep pets that are illegal in their state or locality. They often do so because of the overwhelming bureaucracy that surrounds such pets. Even when you obtain officially published guidelines these may be very difficult to understand. At times they appear to be contradictory, needing a specialist to explain them. Sometimes, you may be referred to a succession of people in other departments until you eventually give up in despair!

THE MAJOR FEDERAL AGENCIES

The Fish and Wildlife Service (FWS), the Department of Natural Resources, and the United States Dept. of Agriculture (USDA) are three of the major federal agencies that are involved in animal-keeping legislation. Laws are enacted for the many reasons, but the following are the most important:

1) To ensure animals traded as pets are maintained under proper standards of husbandry.
2) To ensure animals being kept as pets do not pose a threat to the health of the community.
3) To ensure animals being kept do not pose a threat to native flora and fauna in the event they should escape into the wild.
4) To ensure animals designated as endangered, or even protected, in their country of origin are not illegally imported into the USA for sale as pets.

That these laws are needed is easily illustrated. The introduction of the gray squirrel from North America into Europe had a devastating effect on the native red squirrel. The introduction of the rabbit to Australia proved a very costly mistake. Cats introduced onto certain oceanic islands resulted in extinction of rare bird species. The practice of introducing non-native fish into American waters also had a deleterious effect on some American fish populations. Each year millions of pets are abandoned by so-called pet lovers.

These people display no remorse for the pets they discard, nor any form of responsibility to the community for their senseless acts. If there were no regulations controlling the owning of animals, there would be those who would keep cows and pigs in urban homes. There would be dangerous animals being kept under conditions that were far from satisfactory in regard to care and security.

If you find that a sugar glider may not be legally kept in your locality you must first understand that a few million pet owners before you have contributed to the need to have regulations because of their lack of responsibility. The next thing to appreciate is that regulations tend to be applied to entire blocks of animals, for example cattle, swine and poultry, dangerous to human species, and so on. Federal agencies cannot forecast every animal that may become a popular pet, which is why animal groups are defined. It

then becomes a case of hobbyists changing, by petition, laws that seem inappropriate to that group, or an individual species within it. In the pet industry, for example, the Pet Industry Joint Advisory Council (PIJAC) monitors each year over 8,000 proposed restrictive legislations in one form or another where pets are concerned.

USDA DEFINITION OF THE SUGAR GLIDER

The sugar glider is not specifically named by the USDA within their guidelines for species which they define as "pocket pets." The latter animals are "non dangerous exotic mammals having no special husbandry requirements, and are intended for personal pets." However, it must be assumed that the sugar glider falls within the following USDA guidelines of exotics which do not require licensing for pet shop sale purposes. "This would include, but not be limited to, hedgehogs, degus, spiny mice, prairie dogs, flying squirrels, and jerboas. Hopefully, this will solve the problem that surfaces when an exotic mammal becomes a popular pet."

The USDA is the federal agency that issues regulations on how animals must be cared for if kept for breeding and sale purposes. Their regulations apply on a national basis. It is this agency that issues licenses for breeding and sales if they are appropriate to the individual seller or breeder. We will discuss licensing later in this overview.

FISH & WILDLIFE SERVICE (FWS)

This federal agency operates on a state-by-state basis. It determines which animals can legally be kept as pets. What may apply in New York may not do so in California, and so on. In some states, other federal agencies, such as the Department of Natural Resources, may be involved in legislation. To make matters more complex, even if the Fish and Wildlife Service allows the keeping of a given exotic pet, there could still be county and local ordinances that forbid this.

Your local Fish & Game Department should be your starting point in establishing what the legal position is in your state. You can then check with your town hall, vets, or pet shops to establish if they know of ordinances in your home vicinity. Locally, in most instances, it is unlikely that the sugar glider will have restrictions placed on it if the Fish and Game Department allow it to be kept as a pet–but you should still check this out.

USDA BREEDER LICENSING

If you plan to breed sugar gliders you are advised to obtain a USDA license. A memo issued by the USDA states:

"Selling of these pets directly to the public, presumably as pets, does not require a license. In such situations, the seller is comparable to a retail pet store, and (by policy) retail sale of pocket pets does not require a license. Selling pocket pets for breeding purposes beyond just maintaining a 'private collection' will require a license, since these animals are not sold primarily as pets."

The selling of sugar gliders to someone who is going to sell them will also require licensing. It is therefore best to hold such a license. To obtain this you must contact the Animal Care Sector Office that covers your state. Request an application form and this will detail all requirements (you must be over 18 to apply). In due course, after filing your application, a USDA official will visit to inspect the premises where the sugar gliders are kept. These officials will advise you on any shortcomings. It is prudent not to argue with them. They are simply trying to do their job. You should comply with their requests.

HOW TO CHANGE RESTRICTIVE LAWS

If your state or locality applies a ban on the sugar glider, the only way possible for changes to be made is by petitioning the appropriate department or committee to review the legislation. You will be unable to do this alone. The suggested steps are as follows:

1) Obtain copies of the laws or ordinances so the basis of the restriction can be established.
2) Try to form a local or state lobby group with others who wish to own these pets.
3) Contact a sugar glider association (if one is formed) in order to see if they can provide help.

4) Contact PIJAC and seek their counsel–they may already be actively preparing to petition in your state with a lobby group.

5) Prepare your own document that gives valid reasons why the restrictions are not appropriate. Alternatively, suggest what restrictions could be applied that would address the concerns of the department or committee, while allowing serious hobbyists the opportunity to own these pets.

Always bear in mind that you will not achieve anything simply by contacting the legislator and 'complaining.' Laws are enacted based on detailed information supplied by various sources. These include lobby groups that are opposed to the keeping of any pets. Sometimes, the information supplied is incorrect, or very biased. Only by presenting a constructive petition can laws be changed.

UNITED STATES DEPT. OF AGRICULTURE (USDA) SECTOR OFFICES

North Central Sector
Illinois, Indiana, Iowa, Minnesota, Michigan (Upper Peninsula), Wisconsin, North Dakota, South Dakota, Nebraska:
    USDA, APHIS
    Butler Square West
    Room 625
    100 North Sixth Street
    Minneapolis, MN 55403
    (612) 370-2255

Northeast Sector
Connecticut, Delaware, District of Columbia, Maine, Maryland, Massachusetts, Michigan (Lower Peninsula), New Hampshire, New Jersey, New York, Ohio, Pennsylvania, Rhode Island, Vermont, West Virginia:
    USDA, APHIS
    2568-A Riva Road, Suite 302
    Annapolis, MD 2140-7400
    (301) 962-7463

South Central Sector
Arkansas, Kansas, Louisiana, southern Mississippi, Missouri, Oklahoma, Texas:
    USDA, APHIS
    501 Felix Street, P.O. Box 6258
    Fort Worth, TX 76115
    (817) 885-6923

Southeast Sector
Alabama, Florida, Georgia, Kentucky, northern Mississippi, North Carolina, Puerto Rico, South Carolina, Tennessee, Virginia, Virgin Islands:
    USDA, APHIS
    501 East Polk Street
    Suite 820
    Tampa, FL 33602
    (813) 225-7690

Western Sector
Alaska, Arizona, California, Hawaii, Idaho, Montana, Nevada, New Mexico, Oregon, Utah, Washington, Wyoming:
    USDA, APHIS
    9580 Micron Avenue
    Suite E
    Sacramento, CA 95827
    (916) 551-1561

CUSTOMARY U.S. MEASURES AND EQUIVALENTS
METRIC MEASURES AND EQUIVALENTS

```
1 INCH (IN)                     = 2.54 CM
1 FOOT (FT)      = 12 IN        = .3048 M
1 YARD (YD)      = 3 FT         = .9144 M
1 MILE (MI)      = 1760 YD      = 1.6093 KM
1 NAUTICAL MILE                 = 1.152 MI     = 1.853 KM


1 MILLIMETER (MM)                    = .0394 IN
1 CENTIMETER (CM)               = 10 MM     = .3937 IN
1 METER (M)          = 1000 MM  = 1.0936 YD
1 KILOMETER (KM) = 1000 M       = .6214 MI
```

```
1 SQ CENTIMETER (CM²)           = 100 MM²       = .155 IN²
1 SQ METER (M²)      = 10,000 CM² = 1.196 YD²
1 HECTARE (HA)       = 10,000 M²  = 2.4711 ACRES
1 SQ KILOMETER (KM²)            = 100 HA        = .3861 MI²
```

```
1 SQUARE INCH (IN²)             = 6.4516 CM²
1 SQUARE FOOT (FT²)        = 144 IN²   = .093 M²
1 SQUARE YARD (YD²)        = 9 FT²     = .8361 M²
1 ACRE               = 4840 YD² = 4046.86 M²
1 SQUARE MILE( MI²)            = 640 ACRE        = 2.59 KM²
```

```
1 OUNCE (OZ)  = 437.5 GRAINS = 28.35 G
1 POUND (LB)  = 16 OZ         = .4536 KG
1 SHORT TON   = 2000 LB       = .9072 T
1 LONG TON    = 2240 LB       = 1.0161 T
```

```
1 MILLIGRAM (MG)                = .0154 GRAIN
1 GRAM (G)      = 1000 MG = .0353 OZ
1 KILOGRAM (KG)          = 1000 G         = 2.2046 LB
1 TONNE (T)    = 1000 KG = 1.1023 SHORT TONS
1 TONNE                  = .9842 LONG TON
```

```
1 CUBIC INCH (IN³)              = 16.387 CM³
1 CUBIC FOOT (FT³)              = 1728 IN³   = .028 M³
1 CUBIC YARD (YD³)              = 27 FT³     = .7646 M³
```

```
1 FLUID OUNCE (FL OZ)           = 2.957 CL
1 LIQUID PINT (PT) = 16 FL OZ   = .4732 L
1 LIQUID QUART (QT)             = 2 PT       = .946 L
1 GALLON (GAL)     = 4 QT       = 3.7853 L
```

```
1 DRY PINT                      = .5506 L
1 BUSHEL (BU)      = 64 DRY PT  = 35.2381 L
```

```
1 CUBIC CENTIMETER (CM³)             = .061 IN³
1 CUBIC DECIMETER (DM³)         = 1000 CM³       = .353 FT³
1 CUBIC METER (M³)     = 1000 DM³ = 1.3079 YD³
1 LITER (L)           = 1 DM³    = .2642 GAL
1 HECTOLITER (HL)     = 100 L    = 2.8378 BU
```

CELSIUS° = 5/9 (F° − 32°)   FAHRENHEIT° = 9/5 C° + 32°

INDEX

TS-269